Echoes
of our
Journey

Echoes of our *Journey*

Liturgies of the people

Dorothy McRae-McMahon

The Joint Board of Christian Education
Melbourne

Published by
THE JOINT BOARD OF CHRISTIAN EDUCATION
Second Floor, 10 Queen Street, Melbourne 3000, Australia

ECHOES OF OUR JOURNEY: Liturgies of the people

National Library of Australia
  Cataloguing-in-Publication entry.

Echoes of our journey: liturgies of the people

  Includes index

  ISBN 0 85819 865 7

1 Worship programs. I. McRae-McMahon, Dorothy, 1934–
II. Joint Board of Christian Education.

264

First printed 1993.

Cover and text design: Kelvin Young
Photography: Coo-ee Picture Library, Joy Merritt and Lynn Lancaster
Typsetting: JBCE
Printing: Australian Print Group   JB93/3345

The liturgies in this book are the work of the people of Pitt Street Uniting Church, 264 Pitt Street, Sydney, New South Wales. They were written between the years 1983-1992 during the ministry of the Rev. Dorothy McRae-McMahon.

CONTENTS

Additional resources used in the services

AHB/WOV	*Australian Hymn Book/With One Voice* (Collins Liturgical)
Taizé	Taizé material is found in *Songs and Prayers from Taizé (Rainbow Books); Music from Taizé, Vols I and II (Collins Dove);* and a series of cassettes and CDs
WCC	World Council of Churches material *In Spirit and in Truth* *With all God's people – the new ecumenical prayer cycle* *With all God's people – orders of service*
WPWS	*Woman Prayer, Woman Song* by Miriam Therese Winter (Collins Dove)
ATN	*All Together Now* (Lutheran Publishing House)
SA	*Sing Alleluia* (Collins Liturgical)
FLF	*Faith Looking Forward* (Oxford University Press)

These resources are available from many Christian bookshops and from

Joint Board Bookshop
Second Floor
10 Queen Street
Melbourne 3000
Tel: (03) 629 5076
Fax: (03) 614 8820

*Pitt Street Uniting Church,
in the heart of Sydney.*

'WORSHIP THAT IS ALIVE FOR PEOPLE'

Preparing a service of worship is both challenging and creative; and usually fun! Most people cannot imagine themselves doing it but discover that, in a group, with some guidelines, marvellous things can happen. Whether we are highly literate or not, most of us have ideas to offer and, when we put them all together, there is a richness and freshness which is beyond our expectations.

Congregations made up of people who have the opportunity to prepare worship begin to understand what it is really about. They own their worship and deeply respect the efforts of others to bring something to life. They begin to see worship as a corporate activity rather than something which belongs to the ordained minister. They become participants rather than an often critical audience.

Ministers have to decide whether they will release some of their power to the laity in order to bring this about. Most of us who are clergy find this somewhat threatening at first. We wonder if we will have any role left. We feel anxious about the standards. We wonder whether it will be more work, rather than less, in the end.

At Pitt Street, we have found that these fears are groundless and that the rewards of sharing worship preparation are great. Mostly clergy attend an early meeting of the worship preparation group to listen, add resources and give any guidance needed. We see clergy as having final responsibility for the conduct of worship but we try to hold open to the maximum number of initiatives from the preparatory group.

There are many Sundays when clergy create liturgy or refine or develop old liturgy. There is always plenty for the minister to do. Lay people respect the gifts of the minister that come from training and personal talents in preparing worship. To let go of power is to have it returned to you in the best way.

The liturgies in this book are the fruits of our corporate work as the people of God in this place and we have had a great deal of joy and fulfilment in producing them. We offer them to others as a basis for their work.

Liturgy

Liturgy literally means 'the work of the people'.

Good worship is primarily a focus on the Holy God but it is also a gathering up of all that we are and bringing that into authentic relationship with our God.

Although there is a place for individual devotional life, Christian worship is essentially corporate. It is the Body of Christ, with all its diversity and different gifts, coming before God. It is clear that we have different ways of worshipping God, some of which are experienced in the several denominations of the church. Some people find it most meaningful to participate in very formal styles of worship, others in less formal. Some people are helped by worship which is full of rhythm and sound, others by spaciousness and silences. Some people follow more ancient traditions and some very contemporary forms.

While acknowledging all this as a true response to our various styles of spirituality, many congregations find it good to explore different options, even if one style is predominant. We also discover that if we look below the outward expressions of our worship, there can usually be seen a common pattern or theology. This pattern reflects the way we relate to God in everyday life. It is a ritual echo of our journey and that is why it has been generally sustained through the centuries.

In looking at this traditional order for worship, imagine that you are seeing it as a repeated pattern for the encounter with God – the growing and changing in response to the awareness of who you are before God, the receiving of a new Word and the living out of the changes with the help of God.

A TRADITIONAL ORDER

The Approach to God

- Greeting: of each other.
- Sometimes processional hymn as the worship leaders enter.
- Call to worship or opening sentences:
    where we firmly state with praise and thanksgiving
    that we are in the presence of the Holy God.
- Hymn of praise.
- Confession:

as we come into the presence of God, we know more fully who we are and we name that before God.
- Assurance of pardon:
  even as we know who we are, we also know the assurance of the grace of God.

Ministry of the Word
We receive the Word of God in Scriptures and in preaching – the biblical and contemporary witnesses.
- Reading
  Old Testament
  Sometimes the Psalm
  New Testament (Epistles)
After each reading, the people may like to respond with thanks: 'Thanks be to God'.
- Often a hymn of faith.
- The Gospel.
- The sermon/contemporary witness.
Some congregations and ministers prefer to see the sermon as the contemporary witness – the testimony to our current experience and understanding of God, arising out of our context and placed in encounter with the biblical witness.
1. Read the Bible passages and focus on the Gospel passage.
2. What words or phrases do you hear for the first time or in a fresh way?
3. Why do you think this passage is in the Bible? What did it mean to the people of the time?
4. What does it remind you of in your own life experiences?
5. What does it have to say to us now?
6. What is the gospel for us?

Response to the Word
Having received the Gospel, we make our response in a number of ways:
- Affirmation of faith or creed:
  we state what we now believe.
- Prayers of intercession:
  we ask God's help as we take up our new life.
- Offering:
  we make our offering to God in money and commitment. At this point we may move into the

Eucharist/Holy Communion and also offer to God the
bread and the wine.

The Eucharist/Holy Communion

This is a special response to the Word where we bring the Great
Prayer of Thanksgiving ('Eucharist' means thanksgiving) and
we receive the food for the journey in the life of Jesus Christ –
the elements. We also remember that we are all together in the
journey as we share the bread and the wine in our common
humanness and our common hope.

The Commissioning

- Commissioning hymn
- Blessing and dismissal: we are sent out to be the people of
  God in the world.

These are the most common elements for worship which the
Christian church has sustained over the years. If we look at
them carefully, it is easy to see that they make sense. Most
people preparing worship find that, if they stick to this rhythm,
worship becomes ordered and fulfilling but they are still very
free to develop the authentic style for their own context.
Worship, at its best, does not need to be gimmicky and
experimental. It is the integrity and relevance of what happens
that makes worship real for people.

Setting up a Parish Worship Committee

There are, of course, many models for Parish Worship
Committees. The following is one which we have found works
well.

The committee is composed of the ordained minister(s) plus a
group of lay people who are interested in the oversight of the
worship life of the parish. It is good to have a cross section of
interests and expertise – people who have skills in music, in
liturgy writing, in the general choreography of worship, in
dance, drama and the visual arts.

These people meet once a month and think well ahead. They
look at the lectionary and are aware of church year services (like
Lent, Good Friday, Easter, etc). They decide on particular
themes to run through periods like Lent and Advent and maybe
a particular focus for days like Easter, Pentecost and Christmas.

They look at possible special issue themes for services between the church year dates, for example peace, celebrating the creation, grieving our violence, or parish anniversaries or other special occasions.

The Worship Committee plans these dates at least three months ahead so that appropriate preparation can begin. For each special service the Worship Committee sets up a Task Group of about five people, one or two of whom are experienced and the others being new to worship preparation. This process means that there are more and more people in the congregation beginning to understand the nature of worship and to share in its preparation.

Each Task Group is given guidelines for the preparation, including a time-line for their work.

For the ordinary Sundays, in between the special services, the Worship Committee gradually builds up a body of liturgy from which it selects services (if the congregation is accustomed to using printed, responsive liturgy). It may also leave services for the clergy to prepare during these periods.

The other task of the Worship Committee is to review the worship of the parish, especially any special services and to work on refining liturgies so that they can be more effective and more appropriate for the developing worship life of the parish.

Guidelines for Task Groups preparing a Service of Worship

1. Ask one person to convene the Task Group and give that person approximately three months before the date of the service concerned.

2. The convenor sets a meeting date for the Task Group at least two months before the service is due and invites the other members of the group to meet (about 5-6 people in all). Each member of the group should be given in advance the paper on liturgy and liturgy writing (as in the first sections of this book).

First meeting
- The convenor describes to the Task Group the exact task.
- The group reads the lectionary passages for the service and reflects on them – perhaps sits in silence with closed eyes and is open to new understandings, special images relating

to the passages, feelings about them. Each person writes down any key impressions and shares them with the group.

- The group writes up thoughts on the theme of the particular service:
    - What are the most important things for us about the theme of this service? For example, Good Friday. Look at the Bible passages. Is there something that stands out for this year? (On one occasion it was, for us, the series of human betrayals that led Jesus to the cross. On another occasion, we saw it was the break-down of human community. We built the liturgy around these themes.)
    - Then we need to ask: What is the key Gospel message for this service? (In the first example, we decided that the key gospel message was that God never betrays us and that we live with the hope that God can lead us into more faithful love for each other. On the second occasion, we saw the Gospel as God's power to heal, restore and recreate the wholeness of community.)
- As a group prepares the liturgy, they keep the particular theme in mind.
- The group looks at the general order of service and takes the main elements which need to be worked on – confession, affirmation of faith and intercessions. It works on each one of the themes in mind and after each question, words, phrases and images are written on a sheet.

Affirmation of Faith

For the affirmation of faith the group, remembering the particular theme chosen, shares words, phrases and images about their faith on this occasion, for example following through on the first Good Friday theme (above):

- God – we can trust the God who gave us the creation, God is an unfailing loving parent.
- Jesus Christ – experiences betrayals with us, was not defeated by our betrayals.
- The Holy Spirit – calls us on to new faithfulness, gives us courage in the hard times.

Intercession

In what way do we need God's help in responding to the Gospel?

Here the group reflects on what particular help they need from God in relation to the focus of the service.

Sometimes they think of a particular repeated response by the people – sung or spoken, for example 'Faithful God, may we be faithful too'.

Next step
- Particular members of the group are then given the sheets with the words, phrases and images on them and asked to take them away and attempt to use them to form up one section of the liturgy as a draft for the group. They need not, of course, use every word, phrase or image but are invited to try to bring together as much as creatively possible of the group's ideas.
- Other members of the group are asked to be responsible for other parts of the liturgy – for example call to worship, blessing and dismissal, music – trying to honour the general feeling of the work of the group in what they write.
- The Task Group is then asked:
  - Are there ways, other than words, through which we could bring the Gospel to life in this service? In music, dance, symbol, movement, decor, visual arts?
  - Ideas are noted.
  - In response to these ideas, are there people whom we should invite to help us prepare the service? People are assigned to approach these people.

Second meeting
- Read through draft sections aloud together, adapting so as to achieve:
  - consistent feel throughout liturgy
  - smooth transition between sections
  - total time within limits
  - something which will work without feeling forced.

If there is to be a contribution of drama, dance, etc., it should be clear by this time what is being planned, what is the theme or message, how long it will take. This meeting would consider when it should happen: is it part or all of the call to worship, confession, intercession, witness, etc? One of the artists' group would ideally be present at this meeting.

This is a creative process and very little (if any) draft liturgy will go unchanged. People are not expected to come to this meeting with the final copy, but with a basis from which the group can work.

- Time each section, and note the time for the whole service. Remember that everything tends to take longer than expected. The group will need to work out what can be left out, or where sections or ideas can be combined to tighten it up.
- You may require people to take sections away to work on and to present to a later meeting. It may be helpful for people to work in pairs at this stage.
- It can be a good idea to give the liturgy to someone outside the group to see if it works for someone who has less information than the group.
- Try to present your work in a way that makes it attractive and accessible for the congregation.
- Celebrate the fruits of your work!

Guidelines for writing liturgy

- Words used in liturgy are simple, concrete and in common usage. Adjectives, abstractions and multisyllabic words are used with great care. Fresh words and images can be powerful, bring new insights and connect us with the here-and-now while the familiar dignity of traditional phrases are 'grounding', give a sense of security, remind us we are part of the church universal, coming before the Holy God.
- The language of the liturgy is moderate rather than extreme. The people will then travel with the liturgy, not drop out because the language is too shocking.
- Sentences are simple and short and direct, easily understood. We make strong, clear statements, for example 'Trust God at all times' rather than 'We should trust God all the time'.
- The language of liturgy flows – more like prose poetry than ordinary prose. It is for speaking rather than reading, and has a rhythm which sets the mood. Slow rhythm: quiet and peaceful, sad, reflective; quick, strong rhythm: energy and movement. Repetition of a word, phrase or sentence gives strong rhythm to liturgy, and tends to highlight the material between the repetitions. You can hear this when you read it aloud.
- The acts of worship give liturgy a shape. Calling together, adoration, confession, assurance of pardon, word, affirmation, intercession, offering, commissioning, sending

out (blessing) – those activities have different words and rhythms, and must flow together smoothly. It is the liturgist's task to see that this happens, to be the 'host' for the occasion. The liturgy writers will ensure that the liturgist always has the 'lead' – that is, speaks first after a silence, and has a short connecting sentence to introduce a new act of worship. This often begins 'Let us now...'.

- Each whole liturgy has a unity of theme, a mood, but there is light and shade within this. The worshippers move from joy to sadness or longing, from quiet to times of energy and resolve, from laughter to awe and wonder. The type of language sets the mood, and the liturgist will facilitate this by changing the pace and quality of voice.
- Except for special services, good liturgy has a quality of timelessness. It can be used many times, in many places.
- Things that make it this time, this place, may be added in spontaneous prayer, dance, drama, music, and in The Witness or Sermon. Liturgy is never about 'performance': dancing, acting, poetry and musical items are blended into the liturgy and offered to God as part of the act of worship.
- Be fussy about copyright. This is a legal obligation. It is also a recognition that the creative efforts of others are not to be stolen and unrecognised. Most people are generous with permissions for 'one off' use of their work.
- Having said all this, we now 'have a go'. The best liturgy expresses the freshness and truth of ordinary people. Many of us, faced with the task of writing a short prayer, stare at a sheet of paper for hours or rapidly write two foolscap pages. Perhaps the most demanding part of liturgy writing is the pruning. This is done firmly and sensitively until we arrive at the fresh, bright kernel of what we want to say now in this liturgy.
- Finally, liturgy writing should be fun.

Many of our most moving liturgies have been written by groups whose meetings were often chaotic and hilarious and seemingly irreverent.

While planning one Good Friday Liturgy in this book we started to picture what could go wrong: if the Cross got 'stuck' and wouldn't come out of the stand, or if people dropped stones on each other's toes and started squabbling. We imagined more and more bizarre accidents and became helpless with mirth. Yet this service was most moving and healing, and

holy. The weight of the stones, the sound of the wood and the sheer beauty of the wooden cross lying on a white sheet, sprinkled with rose petals lifted us all into another world, and most of us in the church that day wept for gratitude.
We are left with the impression that God has a strong sense of the ridiculous and loves to see people having a good time together. Let's celebrate that.

Pitt Street Worship Committee

Services for ordinary Sundays

"We experience the holiness of God
in wonder of creation
and endlessness of sky and sea;
in breathless beauty
and quiet bush..."

SUNDAY MORNING WORSHIP 1

GREETING
Leader: Let us worship God.
              The peace of God be with you all.
People: **And also with you.**

PROCESSIONAL HYMN

CALL TO WORSHIP
Leader: In mystery and grandeur
              we see the face of God;
People: **In earthiness and ordinary
              we know the love of Christ.**

Leader: In heights and depths
              and life and death;
People: **The spirit of God is moving among us.**

All: **Let us praise God.**

HYMN OF PRAISE

CONFESSION
Leader: Let us join in our prayer of confession.

              How great is your faithfulness,
              O God of all eternity.
              We race through life,
              so full of our own plans,
              so consumed by our own anxieties,
              and yet you are still there for us
              when we dare to pause
              before your holiness.
People: **Forgive us, O God,
              and bring us to that moment.**

                    (Silence)
Leader: Without defences we come before you,
              ready to know who we are
              and open to the light of your presence.

People: **We are not the people we would like to be;**
             forgive us and heal us, O God.

                          (Silence)

ASSURANCE OF PARDON

Leader: Do not be afraid.
             There is no condemnation
             for those who believe.
             Let God be God.
             Rise up and live in freedom and hope.
             In the name of the Christ,
             Amen.

People: **Amen.**

             Our father in heaven
             hallowed be your Name,
             your kingdom come,
             your will be done
                 on earth as in heaven.
             Give us today our daily bread.
             Forgive us our sins
                 as we forgive those who sin against us.
             Save us in the time of trial
             and deliver us from evil.
             For the kingdom, the power, and the glory
                 are yours
             now and forever. Amen.

THE MINISTRY OF THE WORD

Reader 1:   Hear the Word of God in the Old Testament.

                 (A reading from the Old Testament)

             This is the Word of the Lord.

People: **Thanks be to God.**

Reader 2:   Hear the Word of God in the Letters.

             (A reading from the New Testament Letters)

             This is the Word of the Lord.

People: **Thanks be to God.**

SENDING OUT OF THE CHILDREN

HYMN OF FAITH

Witness: Hear the Word of God in the Gospel.

(A reading from the Gospel)

This is the Word of the Lord.

People: **Thanks be to God.**

THE CONTEMPORARY WITNESS

AFFIRMATION OF FAITH

Leader: In response to the Word,
let us stand and affirm our faith:

All: **We experience the holiness of God**
in wonder of creation
and endlessness of sky and sea;
in breathless beauty
and quiet bush;
in acts of courage
and silent heart.

We know the God in Christ
in gifts of healing
and liberations of life;
in recognitions of love
and callings to serve;
in sufferings for others
and glimpses of grace.

We live from God's Spirit
in moments of faith
in dreams beyond hoping
and in rhythms of new energy.
We name the God who is our centre.
We claim the goodness
that is ours in God.
We announce the truth
that lies in the Gospel.
We believe we are not alone
in our struggle to be the church.

(The people sit.)

PRAYERS OF INTERCESSION

Leader: Let us bring before God our prayers of intercession:

O God, as we look at our world
we are overwhelmed by its need.
But, in the face of that,

25

we ask for peace and justice
in the countries which we now name...

(The people name countries for which they have concern.)

O God, this is our prayer to you.

People: **We believe; Lord, increase our faith.**

Leader: As we look at our country
we long for leadership
which has integrity;
an end to violence and racism
and a new spirit of community.
O God, this is our prayer to you.

People: **We believe; Lord, increase our faith.**

Leader: As we look at our church
we hope for a humble face
turned with love to the world
and a brave witness to your grace.
O God, this is our prayer to you.

People: **We believe; Lord, increase our faith.**

Leader: As we look at ourselves,
we know our need of more energy,
more vision, more love for each other
and a deeper commitment
to live as the people of the Gospel.
Come to us in your life and power.
O God, this is our prayer to you.

People: **We believe; Lord, increase our faith.**

Leader: For you, O God, are the source of all
that is good and beautiful
and we believe you are for us. Amen.

People: **Amen.**

THE OFFERING

Leader: Let us bring our offerings before God.

(The offering is received.)

THE DEDICATION *(all standing)*

Leader: Receive these our gifts, O God.
People: **For we bring them with thankful hearts**
            for all your kindness to us.
            Amen.

COMMISSIONING HYMN

BLESSING AND DISMISSAL

Leader: Go in freedom and faith.
People: **We go with open hearts and minds**
            believing that Christ walks before us.

Leader: May the Holy God
            surprise you on the way,
            the gospel of Christ
            be always real for you,
            and the Spirit be your breath of life.
            Amen.
People: **Amen.**

THREEFOLD AMEN *(AHB/WOV, No. 579)*

SUNDAY MORNING WORSHIP 2

Leader: Let us worship God.

PROCESSIONAL HYMN

CALL TO WORSHIP
Leader: Do you see this city?
           Here God dwells among the people.
People: **God will make a home among us
           and we shall be God's people.**

Leader: God is the beginning and the end
           and is making the whole creation new.
People: **Let us worship together!**

HYMN OF PRAISE

CONFESSION
Leader: In penitence and faith we come before you,
           Holy God, and say: 'This is who we are'.
           We are the people
           who long for the new heaven and the new earth
           but can't always take the first step towards it.
People: **Forgive us, gracious God.**

Leader: We are those who love the city
           but who participate
           in its destructive patterns of life
           and fail to lift up
           its beauty and creativity.
People: **Forgive us, gracious God.**

Leader: We are the people who commit ourselves
           to build the community of the Gospel
           but we so often betray that hope
           and fail each other.
People: **Forgive us, gracious God.**

Leader: We are those who sometimes see the vision
           for our own lives

but we are weak and fall far short
of the dream.

People: **Forgive us, gracious God.**

ASSURANCE OF PARDON

Leader: In Jesus Christ, we may always announce
that now is the time of the new heaven
and the new earth.
The old order has passed away
and the new creation is before us.

People: **Thanks be to God!**

Our Father in heaven,
hallowed be your Name,
your kingdom come,
your will be done
on earth as in heaven.
Give us today our daily bread.
Forgive us our sins
as we forgive those who sin against us.
Save us in the time of trial
and deliver us from evil.
For the kingdom, the power, and the glory
are yours
now and for ever. Amen.

THE MINISTRY OF THE WORD

Reader 1: Hear the Word of God in the Old Testament.

(A reading from the Old Testament)

This is the Word of the Lord.

People: **Thanks be to God.**

Reader 2: Hear the Word of God in the Letters.

(A reading from the New Testament Letters)

This is the Word of the Lord.

People: **Thanks be to God.**

SENDING OUT OF THE CHILDREN

(The children gather at the front.)

Leader: We send you out to learn
that God loves the world
and all its people

29

and that God loves you.
Amen.
People: **Amen.**

HYMN OF FAITH
Witness: Hear the Word of God in the Gospel.

(A reading from the Gospel)

This is the Word of the Lord.
People: **Thanks be to God.**

THE CONTEMPORARY WITNESS

AFFIRMATION OF FAITH
All: **In desert and bushland, mountain and water,**
            we see the signs that God is with us.
            In grass that grows through cities of concrete,
            we see the signs that God is with us.
            In the faces of people whom God so loves,
            we see the signs that God is with us.
            In our brokenness,
            there is the hope of wholeness.
            In our emptiness,
            there is the hope of fullness,
            In our deaths,
            lies the hope of resurrection life.
            This is the Word in Christ to us.
            The flame of the Holy Spirit
            lives in this place
            and travels with us.
            Amen.

PRAYERS OF INTERCESSION
Leader: Let us pray.
            O God, who looked upon the city of Jerusalem
            and wept over it,
            stand with us as we look at our city
            and our world.
People: **For we long to see a new heaven and a new earth.**

Leader: We see the pain and struggle of the people
            bowed down by exploitation and conflict.
            We hear the groaning of the creation
            as it waits for new life and hope.

People: **Make us part of your new creation, O God.**

Leader: We see the city and hear its sounds around us.

(Silence)

We picture its skyline and harbour
in all its beauty
and feel that pulse of its life –
moving and stopping,
despairing and hoping,
laughing and crying,
with all its possibilities for community
and all its possibilities for alienation.
We love our city, gracious God.

People: **Be with us at its heart**
and reveal to us the signs of your presence.

Leader: We see your church,
in all its humnanness,
standing in divided witness still,
struggling to understand
the Gospel for this day and this place.

People: **Recreate us, O God,**
and send to us your liberating Spirit.

Leader: Each one of us, in our own place, O God,
sees the need and hears the cry of humanity.
Let those who will
lift up their prayers for the church
and the world...

(People offer their prayers.)

We see ourselves, O God,
people of faith and faithlessness –
dancing in the sun one day
and overwhelmed by our realities on the next,
joyfully announcing the Gospel sometimes
and then trembling in our uncertainty.
We see the hope that lies among us –
the hope that we could care
and live in community with each other
and the world.

People: **Give life to this hope in us, God of community.**
Bring to us a celebration of all that is,
in its ambiguity, its frailty and its costliness.
Amen.

THE OFFERING
Leader: Let us offer our gifts as a sign
of our commitment to Christ
and the world.

PRAYER OF DEDICATION

(All standing)

Leader: Let us praise God.
People: **O God, who calls us from death to life,**
we give ourselves to you
and with the church through all ages,
we thank you for your saving love
in Jesus Christ.
Amen.

THE COMMISSIONING

COMMISSIONING HYMN

THE BLESSING AND DISMISSAL
Leader: The night shall be no more
and we will need no light from lamps.
People: **For God is our light,**
and always walks before us.

Leader: Go forth into the light
and share in the recreating of the world.
And may God the beginning give you a new day
God the Christ take you by the hand
and God the Spirit give you energy and peace.
Amen.
People: **Amen.**

THREEFOLD AMEN *(AHB/WOV, No. 579)*

SUNDAY MORNING WORSHIP 3

GREETING
Leader: Peace be with you.
People: **And also with you.**

PROCESSIONAL HYMN

CALL TO WORSHIP
Leader: All creation sings with joy:
People: **God is love.**

Leader: Cross and resurrection
            speak the word:
People: **Christ is love.**

Leader: Life that leaps forth
            reminds us again:
People: **The Spirit is love.
            Thanks be to God!**

THE HYMN OF PRAISE

PRAYERS OF THANKSGIVING AND CONFESSION
Leader: Let us reflect on the love of God for us:
            – always moving towards our need
            – unconditionally accepting and gracious
            – participating in our pain and grief
            – releasing us towards new life
            – never leaving us alone
            – forgiving and re-creating.
                        (Silence)
Leader: O God, before your love for us,
            we make our humble confession:
People: **We have not so loved each other.**
                        (Silence)
Leader: By night we travel in darkness.
All: **'By night we travel in darkness'** *(Taizé – sung twice)*

33

ASSURANCE OF PARDON

Leader: Light and dark are both alike to God.
Nothing can separate us
from the love of God in Christ Jesus.
Go forward in faith
because Christ goes before you.
Amen.

All: **Amen.**

THE MINISTRY OF THE WORD

Reader 1:   Hear the Word of God in the Old Testament.

(A reading from the Old Testament)

This is the Word of the Lord.

People: **Thanks be to God.**

Reader 2:   Hear the Word of God in the Letters.

(A reading from the New Testament Letters)

This is the Word of the Lord.

People: **Thanks be to God.**

SENDING OUT OF THE CHILDREN

Leader: We send you out to learn and play together,
to discover the love of God
and your place in the family of the church.
Amen.

People: **Amen.**

HYMN OF FAITH

Witness: Hear the Word of God in the Gospel.

(A reading from the Gospel)

This is the Word of the Lord.

People: **Thanks be to God.**

THE CONTEMPORARY WITNESS

CELEBRATION OF FAITH

Leader: In response to the Word,
let us stand and celebrate our faith:

All: **In harmonies of sun and rain
and smoky bush
with rocky crags;**

in shadows patched with light
on city streets,
we celebrate Creator God.
We celebrate the source of life.
We celebrate with joy the source of love.

Women: God is the beginning.

Men: God is the ending.

All: Our feet are firmly placed on holy ground.

In wrenching moments
harsh with pain;
in love discovered, freedoms won,
in times of humanness
and facing truth,
we celebrate Incarnate God.
We celebrate the Cross of Christ.
We celebrate with joy the risen One.

Men: God is the beginning.

Women: God is the ending.

All: Our feet are firmly placed on holy ground.

In courage found
and wisdom known,
in lifted hearts,
in flights of hope
and unities beyond
the common flow,
we celebrate the Holy Spirit.
We celebrate the go-between.
We celebrate with joy the gifts of God.
God is the beginning.
God is the ending.
Our feet are firmly placed on holy ground.

PRAYERS OF INTERCESSION

Leader: Let us join in our prayers of intercession.

O God,
who listen to us all,
we hear the weeping of the world
as the forests are destroyed,

35

the seas polluted
and the vulnerable creatures threatened.
We pray for new commitment
to restoring your good creation.

People: (*Sung response*):

**'Son of God, O Lord Jesus Christ,
show us your mercy.
Lord, hear our prayer,
Lord, hear our prayer.'** *(Taizé)*

Leader: We hear the weeping of the people
weak with hunger,
bowing under oppression,
fleeing from war.
We pray for new paths
to justice and peace.

People: (*Sung response*)

Leader: We hear the weeping in our midst,
in loneliness,
betrayed hopes,
unrecognised gifts.
We pray for a new love
for each other and our neighbours.

People: (*Sung response*)

Leader: Let those who will
lift up their prayers
for the church and the world...

(*People offer their prayers.*)

We pray for a new heaven
and a new earth.

People: (*Sung response*)

THE OFFERING

Leader: Let us bring our offering before God.

(*The offering is received.*)

THE DEDICATION *(All standing)*

Leader: Receive these our gifts, O God.
People: **They are a sign of our love**
            for you and the world.
            Amen.

THE COMMISSIONING HYMN

BLESSING AND DISMISSAL

Leader: Spread God's love
            beyond this place.
People: **We go in faith**
            and thanksgiving.

Leader: And may the God of love
            give you grace;
            the God in Christ
            give you mercy;
            and the Spirit lift up your hearts.
            Amen.
All: **Amen.**

THREEFOLD AMEN *(AHB/WOV, No. 579)*

SUNDAY MORNING WORSHIP 4

GREETING

Leader: The peace of God be with you.
People: **And also with you.**

PROCESSIONAL HYMN

OPENING SENTENCES

Leader: God looks at the world
and sees that it is good.
People: **Thanks be to God.**

Leader: A world worth dying for,
a world worth living for.
People: **Thanks be to Christ.**

Leader: And we are never left alone
in joy or struggle,
failure or victory.
People: **Thanks be to you, Holy Spirit.**

HYMN OF PRAISE

CONFESSION

Leader: Let us join in our prayers of confession:
O God, you die for us and conquer death for us.
People: **But we find it hard to believe in your love.**

(Silent reflection)

Leader: We see your creativity in all the earth.
People: **But fear to ask for our own healing.**

(Silent reflection)

Leader: We hear your invitation to peace.
People: **But we dare not stop to receive it
in case it is not possible.**

All: **Forgive us and bring us to faith.**

KYRIE *(Sung by all):*

Kyrie eleison, Kyrie eleison, Kyrie eleison. *(WCC)*

ASSURANCE OF PARDON

Leader: Hear the Word to us in Christ.
If we have faith as small as a mustard seed,
God's power is released in us.
Our healing is a gracious gift.
Rise, take up your bed and walk.
Amen.

People: **Amen.**

MINISTRY OF THE WORD

Reader 1:   Hear the Word of God in the Old Testament.

(A reading from the Old Testament)

In this is the Word of the Lord.

People: **Thanks be to God.**

Reader 2:   Hear the word of God in the Letters.

(A reading from the New Testament Letters)

In this is the Word of the Lord.

People: **Thanks be to God.**

SENDING OUT OF THE CHILDREN

Leader: Go to your program to
play and learn together
that God loves you and the world.
Amen.

People: **Amen.**

THE GOSPEL

THE CONTEMPORARY WITNESS

AFFIRMATION OF FAITH

Leader: In response to the Word,
let us stand and affirm our faith.

           We may lift our faces to the light,

People: **For we are God's good creation
and beautiful in the sight of God.**

| Leader: | When we weep, Christ grieves with us. |
| People: | **When we laugh, the Spirit dances with delight.** |

| Leader: | For we are called to life, life that does not lie. |
| People: | **It holds beginnings and endings and much we do not understand.** |

| Leader: | We glimpse its patterns but not as often as we would like. |
| People: | **We know its passionate freedoms and the depths of its betrayals.** |

| Leader: | But in its brokenness, in the wrenching and the bleeding, we find a still, strong centre and the ripples of a rigourous love. |
| People: | **In that we will trust. In that we name our God. In the company of that hope and the power of our community, we will claim our faith in all that stands before us.** |

PRAYERS OF INTERCESSION

Leader: Living God,
we ask you to bless us.
We wait expectantly
for the renewing energy
of your love for us
and for the world.
We open ourselves
to the power of your healing.

(Silent prayer)

O God,
we are deeply concerned
about the people and situations
which we now bring before you.
We ask your blessing on them.

(The people name their concerns.)

Leader:	Breathe your life into us, O God.
People:	**Gather us under the wings**
	of your love
	as a mother hen gathers her chickens.

| Leader: | Comfort our grief. |
| People: | **Ease our pain with your gentleness.** |

Leader:	Lift our hopes
All:	**That we may stand free**
	and take up our life
	with new courage and faith.
	Amen.

'Bless the Lord, my soul' *(Taizé)*

THE OFFERING
| Leader: | Let us bring our offerings |
| | before God. |

(The offering is received.)

DEDICATION *(All standing)*
Leader:	Receive these gifts, O God.
People:	**Bless them that they**
	may be wisely used
	for your work in the world.
	Amen.

COMMISSIONING HYMN

BLESSING AND DISMISSAL

BLESSING SONG

Leader:	Go in peace:
	and may God the Mother keep you safe
	God in Christ take you by the hand
	and God the Spirit cover you with
	her warm bright wings.
	Amen.
People:	**Amen.**

THREEFOLD AMEN *(AHB/WOV, No. 579)*

41

Eucharistic services

"The city sounds with your voice, O God,
in calls for justice and laughter in streets.
The city breathes with your life, O God,
in green grass in concrete,
and new hope in people."

HOLY COMMUNION IN THE CITY

GREETING
Leader: The peace of God be always with you.
People: **And also with you.**

PROCESSIONAL HYMN

CALL TO WORSHIP
Leader: The city reflects your face, O God.
People: **In wrinkles of kindness and hand touching hand.**

Leader: The city sounds with your voice, O God.
People: **In calls for new justice and laughter in streets.**

Leader: The city breathes with your life, O God.
People: **In green grass in concrete,
          and new hope in the people.**

All: **Let us worship God.**

HYMN OF PRAISE

CONFESSION
Leader: Let us be aware of who we are before the holy God.

          (Silent reflection)

          Lord, have mercy.
All: **Lord, have mercy** *(or sung 'Kyrie' – Taizé or WCC))*

Leader: Your will is not yet done in us, O God.
All: **We do not love as you love;
          we bind instead of freeing.
          Our grace is less than your grace,
          and our courage often fails.
          Forgive us and bring us to a new day.
          Amen.**

ASSURANCE OF PARDON
Leader: In the city of God,
          all are forgiven, and called to share

in the building of a new heaven and a new earth.
This is the promise in Christ to us.

All: **Thanks be to God.**

GLORIA

MINISTRY OF THE WORD

READINGS
Reader 1:   Hear the Word of God in the Old Testament.

(A reading from the Old Testament)

This is the Word of the Lord.
People: **Thanks be to God.**

Reader 2:   Hear the Word of God in the Letters.

(A reading freom the New Testament Letters)

This is the Word of the Lord.
People: **Thanks be to God.**

SENDING OUT OF THE CHILDREN
Leader: We send you out as our loved children
             to learn and to play.
             We also send out leaders from among us
             who will care for you on our behalf
             until you return to share with us
             the bread and wine.
             Amen.
All: **Amen.**

HYMN OF FAITH

GOSPEL
After the reading from the Gospel:

Witness: This is the Gospel of the Lord.
People: **Praise to you, Lord Jesus Christ.**

THE CONTEMPORARY WITNESS

AFFIRMATION OF FAITH
Leader: In response to the Word,
             let us stand and affirm our faith.

All: **We believe in God**
whose creativity is not defeated
     by concrete or traffic,
but shines forth in the centre of our life.
We believe in Jesus Christ
who lived as friend and saviour
     to the people of the city,
who ate and laughed
wept and celebrated
with ordinary people like us.
We believe in the Holy Spirit
who dances in the city
     as truth and moments of love,
who goes between us with threads of community
and never leaves us without hope.
And we believe in the church
which is real when it stands open
to the life of the city
and bears witness to the love and justice of God.

INTERCESSION AND LITANY FOR THE CITY

Leader: Let us bring before God the life in the city.
In its loneliness and weariness,
its pain and its brokenness:

People: **breathe healing and energy, O God.**

Leader: In its struggles for meaning
and search for identity:

People: **give courage and purpose, O God.**

Leader: In its longings for new things
and deepest dreaming moments:

People: **send vision and hopefulness, O God.**

Leader: Through us, its people, and the buildings
with which we are gifted:

People: **Bring new love and new freedoms, O God.**

Leader: For we listen to the songs of the city,
in the murmuring rhythms,
rising and falling,
the sounds of the working,
the walking and talking,
sing the songs of the city.

People: **For God is in our midst.**

Leader:	In small patches of sunlight, and flashes of colours flickering and dancing, reflecting and splashing, sing the songs of the city.
People:	**For God is in our midst.**
Leader:	In the faces of lovers and lonely and purposeful, hurrying and dreaming faces from everywhere, sing the songs of the city.
People:	**For God is in our midst.**
Leader:	In the soaring of office towers crowding of old things, tunnels of wind and shrieks of the sirens, sing the songs of the city.
People:	**For God is in our midst.**
Leader:	In the life touching other life, moments of kindness, shout of the protesters, laugh of the garbagemen, sing the songs of the city.
People:	**For God is in our midst.**
Leader:	In awareness of humanness oneness in longing fumbling for deeper things, fragments of hopefulness, sing the songs of the city.
People:	**For God is in our midst.** **Amen.**

SERVICE OF THE EUCHARIST

THE OFFERING

Leader:	Let us bring our offerings before God.

(The offering is received.)

THE DEDICATION *(All standing)*

Leader: We bring our gifts to this table
and join with the hospitality of God.

People: **We bring a gift from our work to share with others.**

(The offering is placed on the table.)

Leader: This bread and wine
are gifts of the work of others
and of the earth itself.

People: **We receive them with thankfulness.
These ordinary things of the world
Christ will make special for us.**

(The bread and wine are placed on the table.)

Leader: Christ is the host for the city
and all who will come are guests at the feast.

GREAT THANKSGIVING *(All standing)*

Leader: Christ be with you.

People: **And also with you.**

Leader: Lift up your hearts.

People: **We lift them to our God.**

Leader: Let us give thanks to the Lord our God.

People: **It is right to give our thanks and praise.**

Leader: We thank you, God,
that you are the beginning
and end of all things
and that you sustain our life
in bushland and city,
mountain and countryside.

People: **We thank you for Jesus Christ
who never turned away from those he met
as he walked the streets of the city,
and who calls us still to take our place
in your kingdom.**

Leader: For this we praise you
with the faithful of every time and place
joining with the whole creation
in the eternal hymn:

All: Holy, holy, holy Lord,
              God of power and might,
              heaven and earth are full of your glory.
              Hosanna in the highest.
              Blessed is he who comes in the name of the Lord.
              Hosanna in the highest.

INSTITUTION

INVOCATION OF THE HOLY SPIRIT

LAMB OF GOD

All: Jesus, Lamb of God, have mercy on us.
              Jesus, bearer of our sins, have mercy on us.
              Jesus, redeemer of the world, grant us your peace.

THE DISTRIBUTION

FINAL PRAYER

All: We thank you that we are the guest at your table,
              O God.
              We pray that, in response,
              we will carry your hospitality
              into the life of this city.
              Amen.

COMMISSIONING HYMN

BLESSING AND DISMISSAL

Leader: Go in peace
              and carry this sacrament into life.
              In brokenness, discover wholeness.
              In the many, find oneness.
              In the centre of our common humanness,
              experience the presence of the living God.
              Amen.
People: Amen.

THREEFOLD AMEN   *(AHB/WOV, No. 579)*

GRIEVING OUR VIOLENCE

GREETING
Leader: In the centre of our grieving for our own violence
and the violence abroad in the world,
we carry in the symbol of the God of light.

THE PROCESSIONAL HYMN
(The candle is carried to the table.)

CALL TO WORSHIP
Leader: God brings light to the world
People: **and the darkness becomes warmed around us.**

Leader: Christ lives beyond our violence
People: **and the power of death is dimmed.**

Leader: The Spirit treads in our footsteps
People: **and the face of a child
invites us to trust.**

HYMN OF PRAISE

PRAYER OF CONFESSION
Leader: As we make our choices,
as we violate each other,
the light of God is hidden.

(The candle is extinguished.)

Let us join in our prayers of confession.

We grieve, O God,
when we see the violence in our community:
between the powerful and defenceless,
rich and poor,
men and women,
adults and children.

People: **We grieve at the anger and pain
in wounded minds and bodies,
the fear in our hearts and our cities,
our loss of hope
in your love and mercy, O God,
in ourselves and in humankind.**

Leader: Too often we have felt paralysed
in moments that call for
acts of courage and kindness...
We have found ourselves
faithless amid suffering
and sometimes choose authorities
whose only answer to society's violence
is institutional violence.

We support media that focus on brutality
entertainments that degrade
and harden us.
We turn some of our neighbours
into stereotypes and scapegoats
and we fail many times to forgive.

People: **We long to control our violence,**
find new ways through,
to love our neighbours as ourselves,
to build community and trust together
and to respond more often with creativity and care.
We long to find again a peace built on justice
without the weapons of war.

ASSURANCE OF PARDON

Leader: Hear the word to us in Jesus Christ:
I am with you always
until the end of the age.
Rise up and live with faith and freedom;
I am making all things new.
Amen.

People: **Amen.**

THE MINISTRY OF THE WORD

Reader 1: Hear the Word of God in the Old Testament.

(A reading from the Old Testament)

This is the Word of the Lord.

People: **Thanks be to God.**

Reader 2: Hear the Word of God in the Letters.

(A reading from the New Testament Letters)

This is the Word of the Lord.

People: **Thanks be to God.**

HYMN OF FAITH

THE GOSPEL

THE CONTEMPORARY WITNESS

AFFIRMATION OF FAITH

Leader: Let us stand and affirm our faith.

All: We believe in the gift of sorrow
            which carries us back to humanness
            and reminds us of the way
            we dreamed life ought to be,
            which marks truly
            our love for people
            and stills us to find new paths
            through the blurred landscape
            of our tears.
            We believe that,
            despite betrayal and deception,
            in a way which we do not always understand,
            we are not left alone.

            And we believe that
            we will not stay sorrowing forever
            but that our spirits will as surely lift
            as the day follows night.

            Despite our doubts,
            we believe that it is always better
            to hope than to despair
            to build anew rather than to destroy
            and to accept that
            life will not confirm our worst fears
            but will surprise us
            with unforeseen revelations.

            God is above us
            God is below us
            God is between us
            God is within us.
            We will not be afraid.

PRAYERS OF INTERCESSION

Leader: Let us join together in our prayers of intercession.

O God, as you wept over Jerusalem,
so we weep over the world in which we live.

(Silence)

O God, help us to work for justice
for the indigenous people of this land,
suffering from white settlement
and the dominance of European culture.

People: **Give us the faith and courage
to accept this responsibility.**

Leader: O God, recreate relationships
between women and men
and give us a sense of hope.

People: **Give us gentleness in our strength
and courage in claiming our lives.**

Leader: O God, renew the lives
of those who are victims of crime
that they may recover a sense of safety and trust.

People: **May the elderly be free of fear,
the poor be given new power
and the rich learn compassion and generosity.**

Leader: O God, give us open arms
for those who flee from violences around the world:
the wars, the tortures and the imprisonments.

People: **May the refugees who come to us for sanctuary
be warmed and encouraged in hope.**

Leader: O God, help us to preserve freedom
when we ask for security,
compassion and equity when we demand justice.

People: **Give us respect for those who are different
and openness to those who model
new possibilities.**

Leader: O God, in this complex world,
we need your strength and your power
to give us hope,
your courage to keep faith
in the future of humanity.

People: **Guide our life, Jesus Christ,**
and set us free.
For you have entered our
innocent suffering
and have risen beyond
our violence.
Amen.

THE SERVICE OF THE EUCHARIST

THE PEACE
Leader: The peace of God be with you.
People: **And also with you.**

(The people exchange the peace.)

THE DEDICATION *(All standing)*
Leader: God who is the source
of everything we are
and everything we have,
People: **we offer you these gifts**
for the people
of our creation.

Leader: We offer you this bread, product of many grains,
crushed to bring forth new life.
People: **God be blessed for all good gifts of creation.**

Leader: We offer you this wine, product of many grapes,
crushed and fermented.
The blood of new life.
People: **God be blessed for all good gifts of creation.**

THE GREAT THANKSGIVING *(All standing)*
Leader: Lift up your hearts!
People: **We lift our hearts to God.**

Leader: Let us give thanks to the living God.
People: **It is good and right to do so.**

Leader: Holy God
we worship you,
author of our innocence,
in rain that falls
on just and unjust world,

in newborn things
which tremble unsecured
before the risks
of all the awful freedoms
in our life.

People: **We worship**
Jesus Christ,
the one who walked
towards our pain
and joined the weeping then
for all that's lost
in our betrayals
of good and truth
and hopeful trust,
and rose reborn to life
and love of us.

Leader: Holy Spirit,
we give you thanks,
strong centre in the brokenness,
the healer of the wounded ones,
present in the struggle
for the grieving and the vulnerable.
Seed of hope
in the face
of our despair.
God in the torn apart,
God in the wholeness,
God in the emptiness,
God in the fullnesses,
we worship you
in songs of never ending praise:

All: **Holy, holy, holy Lord,**
God of power and might,
heaven and earth are full of your glory.
Hosanna in the highest.
Blessed is he who comes in the name of the Lord.
Hosanna in the highest.

THE INSTITUTION

INVOCATION OF THE HOLY SPIRIT

THE MEMORIAL PRAYER

Leader: As we break this bread
and share this wine,

People: **we receive a God
who is at the centre of our brokenness
and the brokenness of the world,
and we drink a cup
which we all hold in common.**

Leader: As we wait in faith
for the healing love of Christ,

People: **we sing of a dream
of reborn hope
and the power of love:
Christ has died
Christ is risen
Christ will come again.**

THE BREAKING OF BREAD

Leader: As the bread is broken,
our brokenness and the brokenness of the world
are one with the brokenness of Christ,

People: **and one with the life of Christ.**

Leader: As the cup is shared,
our bleeding and the bleeding of the world
are one with the dying of Christ,

People: **and one with the life of Christ**

Leader: As the cup is shared,
our bleeding and the bleeding of the world
are one with the dying Christ,

People: **and one with the celebration
of Christ's victory.**

THE DISTRIBUTION

PRAYER OF THANKSGIVING

Leader: Let us share in our final prayer.

All: **We thank you, gracious God,
that we receive life
and food from you
and each other,**

**so that love may be carried
into the world.
We go in faith
to be your people
in the power of your Spirit.
Amen.**

COMMISSIONING HYMN

THE BLESSING

Leader:	God go with you
in all that is gentle.
Christ go with you
in all that is brave;
and the Spirit go with you
in all that is free.
Amen.
People:	**Amen.**

THREEFOLD AMEN *(AHB/WOV, No. 579)*

LITURGY FOR HOLY COMMUNION

GREETING
Leader: The peace of Christ be with you
People: **And also with you.**

PROCESSIONAL HYMN

CALL TO WORSHIP *(All standing)*
Leader: We are always a broken body,
People: **but we are the Body of Christ.**

Leader: With the faithful who go before us,
People: **we are the body of Christ.**

Leader: In Christ is our unity.
            In Christ is our wholeness.
People: **Thanks be to God.**

HYMN OF PRAISE

PRAYERS OF CONFESSION
Leader: As we come before God in confession,
            let us reflect on the symbols at the centre of our life

            (The bread and wine are brought to the table.)

            (Silence)

Leader: In our failure to be the church of love and grace,
People: **we drink a common cup
            and break the common loaf.**

Leader: In our sharing in injustice and violence
            against the people of the world,
People: **we drink a common cup
            and break the common loaf.**

Leader: In our lack of faith and courage
            to follow the way of the cross,
People: **we drink a common cup
            and break the common loaf.**

ASSURANCE OF PARDON

Leader: In our brokenness
and in our humanness,
the Christ is one with us.
In Christ we are set free.
In Christ we are enough to be the church.
Amen.

GLORIA

THE MINISTRY OF THE WORD

Reader 1: Hear the Word of God in the Old Testament.

(A reading from the Old Testament)

This is the Word of the Lord.

People: **Thanks be to God.**

Reader 2: Hear the Word of God in the Letters.

(A reading from the New Testament Letters)

This is the Word of the Lord.

People: **Thanks be to God.**

SENDING OUT OF THE CHILDREN

(The children gather at the front.)

Leader: We send you out together
as our loved children
to learn, to play, as part
of the family of God.

People: **Amen.**

HYMN OF FAITH

Witness: Hear the Word of God in the Gospel.

(A reading from the Gospel)

This is the Word of the Lord.

People: **Thanks be to God.**

THE CONTEMPORARY WITNESS

AFFIRMATION OF FAITH

Leader: In response to the Word
let us stand and affirm our faith.

All: **The people of God**
have a human face.
We laugh,
we weep,
we wait in hope.
We lift our eyes,
and stub our toes,
we love,
and struggle,
we fail
we stand
and always we stand
on trembling ground.

But God is God
and Jesus is the Christ
and the Spirit
will lift up our feet.
God is in the centre,
God is at our endings.
Nothing lies beyond
the love of God in Christ.

PRAYERS OF INTERCESSION

Leader: Let us bring before God
our prayers of intercession.

Come, Holy Spirit, renew the whole creation.
Send the wind and flame
of your transforming life
to lift up the church in this day.
Give wisdom and faith
that we may know
the great hope to which we are called.

People: **Come, Holy Spirit,**
renew the whole creation.

Leader: Spirit of love,
set us free
to emerge as the children of God.
Open our ears
that we may hear the weeping
of your creation.

	Open our mouths that we may be a voice for the voiceless. Open our eyes that we may see your vision of peace and justice. Make us alive with the courage and faith of your prophetic truth.
People:	**Come, Holy Spirit, renew the whole creation.**
Leader:	Spirit of unity, reconcile your people. Give us the wisdom to hold to what we need to be your church. Give us the grace to lay down those things that we can do without. Give us a vision of your breadth and length and height which will challenge our smallness of heart and bring us humbly together.
People:	**Come, Holy Spirit, renew the whole creation.**
Leader:	Spirit of truth, lift up your light among us. May we ever be a true reflection of the gospel and lead the church into honest encounter with itself and the world it claims to serve.
People:	**Come, Holy Spirit, renew the whole creation. Amen.**

OFFERTORY

Leader: Let us bring our offerings to God.

(The offering is received.)

DEDICATION

THE GREAT THANKSGIVING

THE INSTITUTION OF THE LORD'S SUPPER

INVOCATION OF THE HOLY SPIRIT

THE LORD'S PRAYER

THE PEACE

BREAKING OF THE BREAD

THE DISTRIBUTION

PRAYER OF THANKSGIVING

COMMISSIONING HYMN

BLESSING

Leader: May the Holy God surprise you on the way,
            Christ Jesus take you by the hand,
            and the Spirit lift up your feet.
            Amen.
People: **Amen.**

THREEFOLD AMEN *(AHB/WOV, No. 579)*

Pastoral services

"We are the people of hope and faith.
In the Spirit we celebrate our energy
and strength, our power to heal
and our calling to work with God
in the recreating of the world."

WE ARE NOT ALONE

INTRODUCTION

This service is prepared to encourage people who are involved
in the struggle for justice, peace and truth.

OPENING SENTENCES

Let us remember who we are:

Leader: We are the people of dignity.
Down the ages we have been the people of God,
the people who know themselves to be called
to freedom, courage and truth.

People: **We light a white candle for that dignity**
and the power of God in us.

Leader: We are the people who weep
for the suffering of the world.
We are the people who walk with the Christ
towards all who grieve,
who are oppressed and exploited.

People: **We light a purple candle**
for those who suffer with the people
and the power of Christ is in us.

Leader: We are the people of hope and faith.
In the Spirit we celebrate our energy
and strength, our power to heal
and our calling to work with God
in the recreating of the world.

People: **We light a green candle**
for our hope in the Spirit.
We are not alone.

NAMING OUR WEEPING

Leader: Where is the pain in our lives?

(The people name their fears, angers, areas of pain.)

Leader: You are not alone.
People: **Your tears are our tears.**

67

AFFIRMING OUR HOPE

Leader: Who are the people who have given us strength
and courage, who have created models for us?

(The people name the people.)

Leader: These people walk with us.

People: **We have company on the journey.**

THE WORD – Reading from the Bible

AFFIRMATION OF FAITH

Leader: Let us affirm our faith in God:

All: **We believe in God
who created and is creating the earth,
who so loved the world that Christ was sent
to live life with us
and the Spirit to be our strength.**

**God has favoured us and appointed us
to be a light to the peoples
and a beacon for the nations;
to open eyes that are blind,
and release captives from the prisons,
out of the dungeons where they live in darkness.**

**In solidarity with the people of God
around the world,
and in company with the other churches
in this city,
we name ourselves as those who, in Jesus Christ,
are enough to do the task
in this time and this place.
We have heard the call of Christ
to follow in the way of the cross.
In faith we lay down our fear,
our weakness and our lack of worth
and announce again
with those who have gone before us that,
'Where the Spirit of the Lord is, there is liberty'.**

INTERCESSION

Leader: Let us ask God for help along the way:

Response: **'Jesus, remember us'** *(Taizé – sung)*

THE COMMITMENT TO EACH OTHER

(A symbol of common humanness is shared.)

Leader: In the face of all our realities:

All: **We are the people who heal each other,**
           who grow strong together,
           who name the truth,
           who know what it means
           to live in community,
           moving towards a common dream
           for a new heaven and a new earth
           in the power of the love of God,
           the company of Jesus Christ
           and the leading of the Holy Spirit.

BLESSING   *(sung - Taizé or WCC)*

CELEBRATION OF RELATIONSHIP

Leader: Let us worship God.

PROCESSIONAL HYMN

CALL TO WORSHIP
Leader: God is one and God is three:
            creator, redeemer and sustainer.
People: **Let us worship God!**

Leader: Our God is the God of the New Covenant
            and says to us,
            'I will be your God'.
People: **And we will be your people.**
            Let us live as the people of God.

HYMN OF PRAISE

PRAYERS OF CONFESSION
Leader: We are not the people we would like to be
            and we make our confession before you, O God.

            We have given our promise to be your people.
People: **But we turn aside to follow other gods.**
            Forgive us, O God.

Leader: We commit ourselves
            to live in right relationship
            with people of other races,
            people who suffer injustice
            and those who have no power.
People: **But we choose to break that relationship**
            with racism, greed
            and a clinging to our own power.
            Forgive us, O God.

Leader: We pray for the oneness of your church.
People: **But we hold to a sense of pride**
            in our own denomination.
            Forgive us, O God.

Leader:	We claim to be a community of grace and love.
People:	**But we betray that hope** **and fail to care for each other.** **Forgive us, O God.**
Leader:	We make our commitments to each other in love and faith.
People:	**But the complexities of relationship overwhelm us** **and in our human weakness we fail.**
All:	**Forgive us, O God,** **and restore us to right relationship** **with you and with each other.**

ASSURANCE OF PARDON

Leader:	God is faithful to us from the beginning to the end of time. Nothing can separate us from the love of God.
People:	**Thanks be to God.** **Amen.**

MINISTRY OF THE WORD

Reader 1:	Hear the Word of God in the Old Testament.
	(A reading from the Old Testament)
	In this is the Word of the Lord.
People:	**Thanks be to God.**
Reader 2:	Hear the Word of God in the Letters.
	(A reading from the New Testament Letters)
	In this is the Word of the Lord.
People:	**Thanks be to God.**

SENDING OUT OF THE CHILDREN

Leader:	We send you out with those who will care for you on our behalf. You are the children of our love and beautiful gifts of God Amen.
People:	**Amen.**

HYMN OF FAITH

Witness:	Hear the Word of God in the Gospel.
	(A reading from the Gospel)
	In this is the Word of the Lord.
People:	**Thanks be to God.**

THE CONTEMPORARY WITNESS

CELEBRATION OF RELATIONSHIP

BLESSING *(Sung twice)*

All:	**'May the blessing of God**
	go before you...' *(WPWS)*

AFFIRMATION OF FAITH *(All standing)*

Leader:	Let us join together in our affirmation of faith:
All:	**We believe in God the creator,**
	deity, parent,
	and lover of all.
	Nearer than our inner selves,
	yet beyond the boundaries of our imaginings.
	We believe in Christ the redeemer,
	brother to us all
	and Saviour of the world.
	Discovered in the least of people,
	yet mystery of God with us.
	We believe in God's wise Spirit
	permeating our life,
	between and around.
	Passionate as flame and wind
	yet comforter in healing love.
	We believe in the Body of Christ
	called into community
	with God,
	with each other
	and with the whole creation.
	United in humanness,
	confessing and celebrating,
	joined in thanksgiving for grace.

LITANY OF THANKSGIVING AND INTERCESSION

Leader: Let us pray.
           As we walk through the deserts
           and darknesses of life:
People: **We celebrate the faithfulness of God.**

Leader: When our faith falters
           and weakness overcomes us:
People: **We celebrate the faithfulness of God.**

Leader: In the death and resurrection of Jesus Christ:
People: **We celebrate the faithfulness of God.**

Leader: When the church becomes a true community:
People: **We celebrate the faithfulness of God.**

Leader: In the love of two people, one for another:
People: **We celebrate the faithfulness of God.**

Leader: In the dream of a creation
           which is integrated, reconciled and loving:
People: **We celebrate the faithfulness of God.**

Leader: Because our God is faithful to us,
           we bring in confidence
           our prayers of intercession.

           For those who cannot find a loving God in life
           because of oppression and injustice:
People: **Come to them, God of love.**

Leader: For those who cannot believe in love
           because life has been bitter and tragic:
People: **Come to them, God of love.**

Leader: For those who cannot find a loving church:
People: **Come to them, God of love.**

Leader: For those who are alienated and lonely:
People: **Come to them, God of love.**

Leader: For those who cannot love themselves:
People: **Come to them, God of love.**

Leader: And now, let those who will
           lift up their particular prayers
           for the church and the world...

                (People offer their own prayers.)

Leader: Come to them, God of love.
All: **Bring love into the world again, O Christ,
           and use us as loving signs of your grace.
           Amen.**

OFFERING

Leader: Let us bring our offering before God.

                  (The offering is received.)

DEDICATION   *(All standing)*

Leader: Love is more than thoughts and feelings:
People: **We bring you our gifts, O God,
           as part of our commitment
           to live out our love for others.
           Amen.**

COMMISSIONING HYMN

BLESSING AND DISMISSAL

Leader: Peace be with you.
People: **And also with you.**

           (The peace is exchanged with people on either side.)

Leader: Go as the loved children of God
           into the world.
           Live in love with one another
           that the world may believe
           the Christ has come.
           Amen.
All: **Amen.**

LITURGY FOR A HARD JOURNEY

INTRODUCTION

This service was prepared for someone dealing in a painful way with abuse in her early life.

GREETING

Leader: Life is a journey on many different roads

People: **but God is always with us.**

Leader: Sometimes we lift our faces to the sun

People: **and God is with us.**

Leader: But then there is the hard journey
through pathways of pain
and fears in dark places.

People: **But God is with us.**
Nothing can separate us
from the love of God in Christ Jesus.

WHO WE ARE ON THE JOURNEY

Leader: O God who travels with us in the shadows,
you know who we are.
We long for life which is full and free.
We long to know the truth
and we want to leave behind us
all the things which hold us back.

(Silent reflection)

We want to move forward in faith
but the way seems so dangerous
and we stand in helpless fear
before the hiddenness in our past
and in our future.

(Silent reflection)

Leader: Stand beside us, gentle Christ.

People: **Walk before us, brave Jesus.**
Call us on into life, Holy Spirit.
Amen.

WE ARE NOT ALONE

Leader: Hear the Word to us in Jesus Christ:
I will never leave you nor forsake you,
even to the end of time.
I will walk with you
down the pathways of death
and lead you to eternal life.
Amen.

People: **Amen.**

THE WORD: Isaiah 43:1-5; 49:13-16(a)

LIGHTING OF THE CANDLE

Leader: The candle is the sign of the light, warmth and
power of the Holy Spirit.

*(The candle is lit and the person on the hard journey
is asked to come near to the candle.)*

Leader: See the light for your journey
and believe that the Spirit always
moves ahead of you.

Stretch out your hands
and feel the warmth of the flame.
It is the warmth of the love of God for you
and our love for you.
That love will surround you wherever you go.

Take into yourself the power of the Holy Spirit
that you may be given courage
for the next step on the journey.

*(The person on the journey kneels and those present gather around
for the anointing and the laying on of hands.)*

Leader: We are the Body of Christ for you.
As our hands are upon you
so you are one with Jesus Christ
who heals us
comforts us
protects us
and lifts us up to walk forward again.
As we anoint you with the sign of the cross,
we claim the power
of God the loving parent
God in Jesus Christ

and God the Holy Spirit for you.
Receive all these gifts
and claim the life that is before you.

PRAYERS OF INTERCESSION

for the particular person.

(The candle is given to the person.)

THE BLESSING SONG *(Sung)*

All: **'May the blessing of God
go before you...'** *(WPWS)*

SERVICE OF RESTORATION AT THE ENDING OF A MARRIAGE

GREETING
Leader: The grace of our Lord Jesus Christ
and the love of God
and the communion of the Holy Spirit
be with you all.

CONFESSION
Leader: As we prepare to celebrate
the mystery of Christ's love,
let us confess our sin
and ask the Lord for pardon and strength.

Loving God,
when a marriage has ended
we face an experience of death:
– the death of hope for a relationship
– the death of what we thought we saw as our
    future
– the death of an image we had of ourselves
as people who would always
honour the commitment
we made before you and other people.

O God,
we wonder where you were in all of that,
and whether we were wrong in our beginnings
or wrong at our endings.

We come into your presence believing
that we have faced things that were too great for us
and knowing that you never ask us to be destroyed.

We come before you,
the Christ who has entered
all the painful experiences of our life,
and confess that,
in the complexities of human relationship,
we have failed.

We have wounded ourselves and those we love.
Our faith in our own worth and beauty
and in the great possibilities of human relationship
is shaken.

People: **Forgive us, O God.**

Leader: In the depths of our hearts,
we are afraid of our frailty
and our aloneness.

In our brokenness,
we need your healing and your recreating,
your power to restore to us
the hope of the fullness of life.

People: **Forgive us, O God.**

Leader: In the silence
we make our own confession to you.

(Silence)

Leader: Forgive us, O God.
People: **Forgive us and help us, O God.**

ABSOLUTION

(The person concerned kneels and is surrounded by the people.)

Leader: To God
our endings
can be the sign of new beginnings,
our deaths
can be the prelude to the resurrection.
We bear the consequences for what we do,
but we are not condemned.

Receive the gift of new life
and the sign that, even at this moment,
you are one with Christ
who will never leave you
nor forsake you to the end of time.

(Laying on of hands and anointing)

Go in peace,
free forever from all that has gone before.

In the name of God the Creator,
God the Redeemer,
and God the Sustainer.
Amen.

THE MINISTRY OF THE WORD
Psalm 13; Ephesians 2:12-22

Leader: Hear the Word of God in the Gospel:
              'I am come that you might have life
              and have it in all its fullness'.

Leader: Peace be with you.
People: **And also with you.**

(The people share the peace with each other.)

PRAYER OF INTERCESSION

Leader: Gracious God,
              in you we see the promise of all that is new.

We see the barren earth grow green in the spring
and new leaves when the winter has passed.

We watch those who have been brought low
by overwhelming powers of oppression
rise up and live out their destiny as children of God;
and the generations of humanity living and dying,
    struggling and failing,
    despairing and hoping,
held safe by the rock of your faithfulness to us
through the ages.

We pray for all
who grieve a loss in their lives today,
    may they be comforted;
for all who are bowed down by guilt and pain
and for all who look to the future
with fear and loneliness,
    may they experience your loving presence.

We pray for the church that it will,
when any of us are weak and failing,
bear witness to the joy of human relationship
and the beauty of our humanness.

(Followed by prayer specifically relating to the person concerned.)

CELEBRATION OF EUCHARIST

AFTER THE DISTRIBUTION

*A common cup may be used which is, at the end of the distribution of
the elements, presented to the divorced person with these words:*

'Take this cup.
It is a common cup and we give it to you
as a reminder of our common humanness.
Your life is a part of our life and,
in our common brokenness,
we are all dependent on the grace of God.
Keep it as a sign that you are forgiven
and free to live again in faith, hope and love.
Amen.'

THE DISMISSAL

FINAL PRAYER

THE BLESSING

Leader: May the God of peace
           be found within you;
           the God of love
           surround and hold you;
           and the God of liberation
           lift you and bring you new life.
All: **Amen.**

SERVICE OF HEALING

THE WITNESS

Leader: In Jesus Christ, we hear the Good News
that God is like a mother hen
who shelters her chickens
under her warm wings.

People: **We believe that God is love.**

Leader: In Jesus, we see a God
who wept for the people of the world,

People: **and weeps for our wounding.**

Leader: In Jesus, we see a God
who reaches out with healing hands,

People: **who sees our pain and makes us whole.**

CONFESSION

Leader: Let us join in our prayers of confession:
O God, you die for us and conquer death for us,

People: **but we find it hard to believe in your love.**

Leader: We see your creativity in all the earth,

People: **but fear to ask for our own healing.**

All: **Forgive us and bring us to faith.**

ASSURANCE OF PARDON

Leader: Hear the word to us in Christ:
If we have faith as small as a mustard seed,
God's power is released in us.
Our healing is a gracious gift.
Rise, take up your bed and walk.
Amen.

People: **Amen.**

MINISTRY OF THE WORD

Old Testament: Psalm 13
Gospel: Luke 8:43-48

THE CONTEMPORARY WITNESS

PRAYERS OF INTERCESSION

Leader: O God, we cry to you in our anger
that people hurt each other.
People: **Be with us and heal us, O God.**

Leader: We feel the fear and pain
of an innocent and trusting child.
People: **Be with us and heal us, O God.**

Leader: We carry with us the things
that have been done to us
which hurt and destroy.
People: **Be with us and heal us, O God.**

Leader: They stand before us
and weigh us down.
They stop us living with joy and hope.
People: **Be with us and heal us, O God.**

Leader: Lift us up
on the wings of your Spirit.
People: **Set us free with your peace
and your power.**

Leader: For you are stronger
than all the forces that stand against us.
People: **Set us free,
heal our wounds,
O God who never leaves us
nor forsakes us.
Amen.**

THE LAYING OF HANDS

(The person seeking healing kneels.)

Minister: We lay our hands upon you
in the name of Jesus Christ,
healer and lover of the world.

(Silent prayer)

May the Lord of love,
who is more powerful
than all those who would harm us,
give you healing for all that is past
and peace for all that is to come.

May she surround you
with comfort and warmth
and fill you with life
that is stronger than death.
Amen.

People: **Amen.**

THE ANOINTING

Minister: Lift your face to the light.
You are beautiful in the sight of God.
The mark of Christ is upon you;
walk free and open your heart to life,
for Christ walks with you
into a new day.
Amen.

People: **Amen.**

SHARING OF THE COMMON CUP

The cup is passed between the people with the words:

People: **We share life with you.**

After the cup is shared, the minister says:

Minister: Take this up as a sign
of our community with you.
Your tears are our tears;
your hope is our hope;
your prayer is our prayer;
you are not alone.

THE PEACE

Leader: The peace of God be with you all.
People: **And also with you.**

BLESSING AND DISMISSAL

All: **'May the blessing of God
go before you...'** *(WPWS)*

Leader: Go in peace
and may God the Mother keep you safe;
God in Christ take you by the hand;
and God the Spirit cover you
with her warm bright wings
Amen.

People: **Amen.**

Services for the church year

"Among us the Spirit of God conceives new life,
and we feel the life within us.
In our history the Christ makes gentle entry,
and we see the light before us.
Within our dreams the truth of God is revealed;
we await the hope of the world."

LITURGY FOR ADVENT

Leader: Let us worship God.

PROCESSIONAL HYMN

CALL TO WORSHIP
Leader: Among us the Spirit of God conceives new life,
People: **and we feel the life within us.**

Leader: In our history the Christ makes gentle entry,
People: **and we see the light before us.**

Leader: Within our dreams the truth of our God is revealed;
People: **we await the hope of the world.**

HYMN OF PRAISE

LIGHTING OF THE ADVENT CANDLE
Leader: Mary of Nazareth,
            flowing bravely
            with all the possibilities
            for life,
            touching close the deep centres
            of being,
            and present to the Holy Spirit
            of God,
            creating and moving
            and bursting through
            membranes of pain and doubt,
            through labour-filled passages
            into the light
            of the star-shine world –
            and the poor, who kneel in hope
            before the sign of God.

(The candle is lit.)

People: **O God, give to us all the eyes and heart of Mary,**
            who saw the vision for the liberation of the world,

**and with love and courage committed herself
to live out that hope.
Amen.**

PRAYERS OF CONFESSION
Leader: In silence,
            let us reflect on moments in our own lives
            and in the life of the church
            when we have experienced
            the life-giving movement of the Holy Spirit
            and have allowed it to die –
            moments when we have had
            a sense of grief about ourselves,
            a sense of betraying our own possibilities.

                         (Silent reflection)

            In weakness,
            in smallness of hope,
            in vulnerable faith,
            we stand before you, O God.
People: **We come in penitence
            and await your renewing Spirit.**

ASSURANCE OF PARDON
Leader: Where the Spirit of the Lord is,
            there is liberty.
            God is always faithful to us
            and gives to us a new day.
            Amen.
People: **Amen.**

MINISTRY OF THE WORD
Reader 1:   Hear the Word of God in the Old Testament.

                (A reading from the Old Testament)

            This is the Word of the Lord.
People: **Thanks be to God.**

Reader 2:   Hear the Word of God in the Letters.

                (A reading from the New Testament Letters)

            This is the Word of the Lord.
People: **Thanks be to God.**

HYMN OF FAITH
Witness: Hear the Word of God in the Gospel.

(A reading from the Gospel)

This is the Word of the Lord.
People: **Thanks be to God.**

THE CONTEMPORARY WITNESS

THE AFFIRMATION OF FAITH

Leader: Let us stand and affirm our faith.

All: **We believe in God**
    who lives and speaks in sunsets,
    in love-wrapped gifts,
    and fleeting butterflies;
   in women weeping strongly
    for stillborn dreams
    and hopes they never conceived.
   We believe in God,
    indwelling wholly,
    suffering and celebration.

   We believe in Christ,
    honouring our humanness,
   who took nourishment
    from a woman's breasts;
   who climbed trees,
    skinned knees;
   who laughed and cried,
    loved and wept,
    bled and died.
   We believe in the Christ,
    sanctifying life, and death.

   We believe in the Spirit,
    mystically joining us
    to peoples everywhere;
   who intercedes
    with sighs and groans
    too deep for words;
   a shared consuming struggle
    blending our will to God.
   We believe in the Holy Spirit
    incorporating us
    into Christ.

We believe in the church,
    being and becoming,
chosen as God's presence in the world
    despite its frailty
        its foolishness
        its failings.
We believe in the church,
    seeking, however imperfectly,
        to act justly,
        love mercy,
        and walk humbly with our God.

PRAYERS OF INTERCESSION

Leader: Let us join together in our prayers of intercession.

           Our loving Parent, God,
           who can be Mother as well as Father,
           grant us the ability
               to be constantly aware
               that we are always in your presence.

People: **You are the Ground of our Being.**

Leader: We thank you for your presence in the world
           that in our pain and anguish,
               dance and song,
           you are there.

People: **You are the Ground of our Being.**
           Everything that is.

Leader: We remember those
           for whom life seems unbearable;
           for those whose spirit
           weighs them down near death.
           May they find in you
           a hope that will sustain them.

People: **You are the Ground of our Being.**
           Everything that is –
               is because of you.

Leader: We thank you for the gift
               which enables us
           to see and hear
           to think, and feel, and smell –
               the suffering, the poverty, and oppression

of our brothers and our sisters everywhere.
May your Spirit ever move us
    to bring their lives before you
    in love, in action, and in prayer.

People: **You are the Ground of our Being.**
    Everything that is –
        is because of you.
    May we ever be
        the expression of your presence
        in the world.

Leader: And now, let those who will,
    lift up their prayers for the church
    and the world...

        (The people make their prayers.)

Leader: O God, we have come before you
        bringing our hopes and our fears.
    We have come because you have called us
        that we might experience afresh
        your grace and peace.
    Amen.

All: **Amen.**

THE OFFERING

Leader: Let us bring our offering before God.

THE DEDICATION *(All standing)*

Leader: As Mary offered herself in her humanness,
    so we offer our gifts to you, O God.

People: **We bring them in faith.**
    We bring them in gratitude
    for all that we have received.

All: **Amen.**

THE DISMISSAL

Leader: Rejoice in Bethlehem,
        two thousand years ago.

People: **Rejoice in the life**
        that was conceived
            lived
        and given for us.

Leader: Go in peace
          to love and serve the world
          and may God go before you,
          Christ Jesus walk with you
          and the Spirit lift up your feet.
          Amen.
People: **Amen.**

THREEFOLD AMEN *(AHB/WOV, No. 579)*

LITURGY FOR GOOD FRIDAY 1

(The cross stands upright in the front of the church.
A bowl of rose petals is on a table nearby.
A white sheet is folded on a front seat.
A tub of good-sized stones is near the centre of the church.
The centre aisle is wide enough for people to move easily around the
cross when it is placed flat on the floor.)

INTRODUCTION
In this service for Good Friday, we will use periods of silence
and Taizé chants which are repeated, often many times, so we
have time for reflection and meditation. Please feel free to move
about, in the music, finding your own level of harmony. Move
about the worship space, finding the place that feels right for
you. Sometimes the people are invited to move and take part in
a ritual. Please feel free to join in or to stay quietly in your seat.

GREETING
Leader: We gather again on this Good Friday
            at the foot of the cross
            which calls us on,
                not in shame,
                not in fear
            but more deeply into the costly journey
                towards life.
            There is wounding,
            there is weeping.
            In Jesus Christ,
            God is not separated from that.

PROCESSIONAL HYMN: 'O Sacred Head' *(AHB/WOV)*

CALL TO WORSHIP
Leader: In the shadow of our suffering
People: **is the suffering of Jesus.**

Leader: In the shadow of our weakness
People: **is the vulnerability of the Christ.**

| Leader: | In the shadow of our pain |
| People: | **is the God who cried out.** |

| Leader: | We are never rejected, |
| People: | **we are never left alone** |

CHANT: 'By night we travel in darkness' *(Taizé)*

MOVING CLOSER TOWARDS OURSELVES
First Reading: Luke 23:1-32

Leader: God in Christ,
           you travel with us in faith
               towards the hard places in our souls.
           You know the agony of pain, guilt and hurt
               deep within us.
           You know our own frightened faces,
               often hidden from ourselves.
           You know the violence sometimes hurled in anger
           because we feel powerless to take
               the smallest step to freedom.
           You know the grief sometimes lying there
           embalmed and perfumed
           by our resolve
           to remain victims forever.

           There are stumbling blocks within ourselves
           in our travelling, O God.
           We take these stones and lay them
           at the foot of your cross
           which is able to bear the weight
           and the wounding for us.

*(The people take stones to represent their hard things, bring them
forward and leave them at the foot of the cross.)*

CHANT: 'By night we travel in darkness' *(Taizé)*

(Silence)

Leader: We leave these hard things here on our way
           through to life.

(Silence)

Second Reading: Luke 23:33-54
Reader: *reads Luke 23:33-48, then says,* 'All his friends stood
           at a distance, and they saw all this happen.'

94

(Four people lift the cross from its stand, and hold it like a coffin.)

Reader: When it was evening, there came a rich man of Arimathea, called Joseph, who had become a disciple of Jesus. He went to Pilate and asked for the body of Jesus: it was handed over to him.

(Two people lay out the shroud in the middle of the church.)

Reader: Joseph took the body, wrapped it in a clean shroud, and put it in his own new tomb which he had hewn out of the rock.

CHANT: 'O Christe Domine Jesu' *(Taizé)*

(This chant continues while the bearers carry the cross down into the church and place it on the shroud.)

THE CONTEMPORARY WITNESS

(Short silence)

Reader: Near the cross of Jesus stood his mother and his mother's sister, and Mary the wife of Clopas, and Mary of Magdala. Many women were there watching from a distance. Among them were the mother of Zebedee's sons, and Joanna, and Mary the mother of James and Joseph.

These women, who had travelled with Jesus from Galilee and looked after him, were following behind.

Leader: Mary watched the death of her innocent child and held him in her arms.

(A woman takes rose petals from the bowl, and walks down to let them fall on the cross.)

Leader: We remember the death of our innocent selves. We remember the death of innocent, fragile things in the world around us.

CHANT:' O Christe Domine Jesu' *(Taizé)*

(People take rose petals to the cross and touch it.)

Leader: It is time to leave this place. Jesus said 'Father, into your hands I commend my spirit'.

CHANT: 'In our darkness' *(Taizé)*

AFFIRMATION OF FAITH

Leader: As we also commend ourselves into the hands of
God, let us say what we believe.

All: **We believe in God.**
When there was nothing but an ocean of tears,
God sighed over the waters
and dreamed a small dream:
light in the darkness
a small planet in space.

We believe in Jesus Christ.
When hate and fear were raging,
when love was beaten down,
when hope was nailed and left to die,
Christ entered into our deep secret places
and went down into our death to find us.

We believe in the Holy Spirit
who weeps with us in our despair,
who breathes on prison doors,
never admitting it's hopeless,
always expecting the bars to bend and sway
and break forth into blossom.

Reader: They took note of the tomb
and of the position of the body.

Then they returned and prepared spices and
ointments. And on the Sabbath day they rested.

SENDING OUT

Leader: I send you out into the world
in the power of the spirit of Christ
to walk through darkness and uncertainty
towards the joy of Easter Day.
Go in peace.

CHANT: 'My peace I leave you' *(Taizé)*

SERVICE FOR GOOD FRIDAY 2

'Our betrayals and the faithfulness of God'

CALL TO WORSHIP

Leader: Jesus the Christ set his face to go to Jerusalem for us.
People: **Let us worship God.**

PROCESSIONAL HYMN

INVITATION TO ENTER GOOD FRIDAY

Leader: Our God chose to join us
in the crying of humanity.
Do you choose to follow?

People: **We choose to follow Christ
and experience that sorrow.**

Leader: Our God chose to help us
understand the agony of death.
Do you choose to follow?

People: **We choose to follow Christ
and experience that sorrow.**

Leader: Our God gives us the gift of choice
between the narrow gate and the broad.
Which do you choose?

People: **We choose to follow Christ
through the narrow gate
and there we will find life.**

All: **Let us follow the Christ
and witness the choice of life through death.**

THE JOURNEY TO THE CROSS

THE CHOICE FACING JUDAS
John 18:1-6

THE RESPONSE

Leader: We often choose to turn from the truth.
We often choose to blind ourselves to the light.

People: **As with Judas,**
            the choice is always before us,
            to trust, or to betray.
            Forgive us, Lord, when we choose to betray.

THE CHOICE FACING PETER
John 18:7-11, 15-18, 25-27

THE RESPONSE

Leader: We often choose to turn from the truth.
            We often choose to blind ourselves to the light.
People: **As with Peter,**
            the choice is always before us,
            to proclaim the truth, or to deny it.
            Forgive us, Lord, when we choose to deny you.

HYMN

THE CHOICE FACING PILATE
John 18:28 to 19:13; 19:17-22

THE RESPONSE

Leader: We often choose to turn from the truth.
            We often choose to blind ourselves to the light.
People: **As with Pilate,**
            the choice is always before us,
            to stand firm for what is right,
            or to try to please everyone.
            Forgive us, Lord, when,
            in trying to please everyone,
            we do what is wrong.

THE CHOICE FACING THE CROWDS

THE RESPONSE

Leader: We often choose to turn from the truth.
            We often choose to blind ourselves to the light.
People: **As with members of the crowd,**
            the choice is always before us,
            to call for justice, or to condemn those whose lives
            we do not understand.
            Forgive us, Lord, when we condemn others.

ORGAN REFLECTION

THE CHOICE FACING THE WOMEN AND JOHN
John 19:25-27

THE RESPONSE

Leader: We often choose to turn from the truth.
              We often choose to blind ourselves to the light.

People: **As with Mary and John,
the choice is always before us,
to take up our responsibilities
or to walk away from them.
Help us, Lord, to take up our responsibilities
to each other, to all we meet,
and to our world.**

THE WORD TO US

Leader: Hear the Word to us in Christ:

              In the face of all our decisions,
all our denials and all our betrayals,
God chooses for us.
God will never leave us or forsake us.
God calls us forth
to the light of Easter Day.

People: **Thanks be to God.**

SONG: 'Santo, santo, santo' (*sung twice* – WCC)

AFFIRMATION OF FAITH

Leader: In response to the Word,
and to the human choices facing us,
let us stand and say what we believe:

All: **We believe in a God who does not betray us,
but who loves and trusts us as a parent.
We believe in Christ
who did not deny the truth,
but followed it even to the cross,
and stands as our truth today.
We believe in the Holy Spirit,
who does not avoid difficult choices,
but who blows like the wind to guide us.
We believe in the witness of Jesus' mother Mary,
the witnesses of Mary Magdalene, Mary and John,**

and those of all the saints
who have gone before us.

We affirm our own humanness.
We choose to follow in response
to this great hope.

INTERCESSION

Leader: Let us join in our prayers of intercession:

Christ of the Cross, break through our boundaries
People: **when there seem to be no choices at all.**

Leader: Christ of the cross, stand before oppressors
People: **and stand beside all who feel overcome.**

Leader: Christ of the cross, lead us on into life –
People: **life which is brave and free
and beyond where we thought we could go.
Lead us to Easter Day.
Lead us to resurrection life.
Amen.**

THE OFFERING

Leader: Let us bring our offerings to God.

(The offering is received.)

THE DEDICATION

Leader: These are the gifts we offer, O God.
People: **We bring them with grateful hearts
in response to all that you have offered to us.
Amen.**

COMMISSIONING HYMN

BLESSING AND DISMISSAL Isaiah 52:11-15

Leader: Depart, then.
Go from here
and choose to bear the vessels of the Lord.
People: **As Isaiah prophesied,
God's servant would cause astonishment,
his visage and form more marred than any other.**

Leader: But he would sprinkle many nations;
rulers would shut their mouths at him

for that which had not been told them
shall they see,
and that which they had not heard
shall they consider.

Go then and consider
what we have witnessed here today.
Go and contemplate the choices placed before us.

People: **We will go, carrying the seeds of hope**
            given to us by those who were last at the cross.

Leader: Go not with haste,
            nor by flight,
            and may the Lord go before you
            and the God of Israel be your reward.
            Amen.

People: **Amen.**

THREEFOLD AMEN   *(AHB/WOV, No. 579)*

LITURGY FOR GOOD FRIDAY 3

This good Friday service explored wholeness and brokenness of community. We used the symbols of fine threads, that when woven together, are strong and whole.

The task group decided that threads (long coloured ribbon) should be woven through the congregation during The Approach. The threads symbolised the 'essentials' that hold a community together.

As we moved through the confession, a ribbon was cut at each point. The fragmented community was one of the 'deaths' we acknowledged during this Good Friday.

The announcement of forgiveness and new life was ensured in the Easter Sunday liturgy. Long trails of ribbon were taken from the cross, and carried by children until they joined around the Eucharist circle.

Leader: Let us worship God.

PROCESSIONAL HYMN: 'O come and mourn with me awhile' *(AHB/WOV, No. 267, verses 1 and 2)*

CALL TO WORSHIP

Leader: Enter the cry in the loneliness
People: **and hear our God.**

Leader: Enter the agony of human pain
People: **and find the Christ.**

Leader: Enter the centre of death
People: **and see our God**

All: **Let us worship God.**

HYMN OF PRAISE: 'O sacred head sore wounded' *(AHB/WOV, No. 255)*

THE APPROACH

Leader: Trust is a ribbon that ties us to one another.
People: **We weave the thread of trust**
through the cloth of our community.

Leader: A thread of courage ties the weak to the strong.

People:	**We weave the thread of courage through the cloth of our community.**
Leader:	There is a ribbon of commitment that binds our community together.
People:	**We weave the thread of commitment through the cloth of our community.**
Leader:	The power of Jesus threads through us and empowers us all.
People:	**We weave the thread of power through the cloth of our community.**
Leader:	Hope is a thread that leads us towards the vision of the kingdom.
People:	**We weave the thread of hope through the cloth of our community.**
All:	**Threads of trust, courage, commitment, power and hope.** **All these we weave through the cloth of our community.**

PRAYERS OF CONFESSION
First Reading: John 18:1-9

Leader:	Dear God, like Judas, we accept positions of trust in our community; but sometimes we abuse that trust, betraying the visions and actions of others, as we pretend to support them, even with a kiss.

(The thread is cut.)

	The thread is broken.
People:	**Forgive us, O God,** **when we break the thread of trust.**

Second Reading: Mark 14:48-52

Leader:	Like the disciples, we have courage if someone will lead us in our task; but often we retreat in fear, when the responsibility falls to us.

(The thread is cut.)

103

The thread is broken.

People: **Forgive us, O God,**
when we break the thread of courage.

Third Reading: John 18:15-18, 25-27

Leader: Like Peter, we announce
that we will be committed to you,
even when it means great cost;
but when we come face to face
with even a small cost,
we often deny you,
and deny you, and deny you again.

(The thread is cut.)

The thread is broken.

People: **Forgive us, O God,**
when we break the thread of commitment.

Fourth Reading: John 18:12-14, 19-24

Leader: We pray that 'your kingdom will come' and that
'The meek shall inherit the earth', but often, like the
Jewish authorities, when we see Jesus empowering
others, we fear the loss of our own power.

(The thread is cut.)

The thread is broken.

People: **Forgive us, O God,**
when we break the thread of your empowerment.

Fifth Reading: John 19:4-16

Leader: Like the crowd,
we are carried along by waves of hope;
but when the tide turns,
we abandon our vision,
and call for the downfall of the visionaries.

(The thread is cut.)

The thread is broken.

People: **Forgive us, O God,**
when we break the thread of hope.

ORGAN: Pachelbel's Canon

(Reflection)

THE CONTEMPORARY WITNESS

HYMN OF FAITH: 'When joy is drowned' *(FLF, No. 33)*

AFFIRMATION OF FAITH
AND ASSURANCE OF PARDON

Leader: Let us stand and affirm our faith and our
            confidence in the unconditional love of God.

All: **We believe in a God who always surprises us,**
            who creates life from death,
            who brings good out of evil,
            who leads us from despair to hope.

            We believe in a God who is faithful to us,
            who shows mercy when we run away,
            who shows patience when we deny the truth,
            who gives reconciling love when we betray.

            We believe in a God who lived and died
            **   as one of us**
            to take the fear out of living and dying,
            to open our eyes to death, within us and around us,
            and open our hearts to new ways of living.

            We believe in a God who forgives us,
            who sets us free from past grief and failure
            and calls us forth into a new day.

PRAYERS OF INTERCESSION

Leader: In our humanness,
            in our brokenness,
            we participate in the cross of Jesus Christ.

            Let us come before God
            in our prayers of intercession:

            Warp and weft we weave
People: **a fragile fabric of humanity**
            bound in common thread.

Voice 1:   This cloth is torn!
            We see those who suffer
            because of their colour,
            their culture, their creed:
            victims of apartheid in South Africa,
            Tamils in Sri Lanka,

Aborigines in Australia,
migrant children in Sydney.
We draw out the differences,
we weave the hate.
We fail to celebrate the common threads
of our humanity.

Leader: This cross stands sharp before us.
Jesus, remember them.

People: **Jesus, remember them** *(sung – Taizé)*

Leader: Warp and weft we weave
People: **a fragile fabric of community
bound in common thread.**

Voice 2: This cloth is torn!
We see more refugee people
than ever before in our history:
from Vietnam, El Salvador,
Africa and the Middle East.
We see people, driven from their homelands
by war and oppression, living fragile from
day to day in refugee camps, depending on
the compassion of the world.

Leader: This cross stands sharp before us.
Jesus, remember them.

People: **Jesus, remember them** *(sung – Taizé)*

Leader: Warp and weft we weave
People: **a fragile fabric of community
bound in common thread.**

Voice 3: This cloth is torn!
In the homeless young who wander our streets,
separated from the love and nurture
which was in the hope and promise of their birth,
failed by our community
when their first home life breaks down.

Leader: The cross stands sharp among us.
Jesus, remember them.

People: **Jesus, remember them** *(sung – Taizé)*

Leader: Warp and weft we weave

People: **A fragile fabric of community
              bound in common thread.**

Voice 4:   The cloth is torn!
              We feel the violation of those who are
              lonely and grieving,
              who need support,
              a compassionate hand,
              the gift of time and friendship.
              So often they receive the promise
              and so rarely the gift.

Leader: This cross stands sharply
              in our midst.
              Jesus, remember us.
People: **Jesus, remember us** *(sung – Taizé)*

THE OFFERING
Leader: The Christ is before us,
              God's gift to the world.
              Let us bring our own gifts before God.

              (The offering is received.)

THE DEDICATION *(all standing)*
Leader: Before your love for us, O God,
              our gifts are small.
People: **But we offer them to you with the prayer
              that you will take them
              and use them
              with love for the world.
              Amen.**

COMMISSIONING HYMN: 'In the cross of Christ I glory'
(AHB/WOV, No. 265)

              (The cross is carried out of the church.)

BLESSING AND DISMISSAL
Leader: Follow the cross towards Easter Day.
People: **There is no other path to life.**

Leader: May the hand of God
              be stretched out to meet you,
              the courage of Christ
              carry you beyond the known way,

and the Spirit gather you up
in the solidarity of love.
Amen.

People: **Amen.**

THREEFOLD AMEN *(AHB/WOV, No. 579)*

LITURGY FOR PENTECOST

Leader: Let us worship God

PROCESSIONAL HYMN

OPENING SENTENCES

Leader: It is time!
People: **Spirit, move in the belly of God,
come, warm into the rock of our beginnings,
alive with original blessings.**

Leader: Spirit, run in the streets of the city.
People: **Flow to the deep brown roots of our belonging.**

Leader: Spirit, invade the air.
People: **Stretch widely with whispering wings,
and cover us with your healing.**

Leader: Spirit, soar in the high towers and shop-fronts.
People: **Carry the seed,
call the song
of the dance in the heart of God.
Wake us to hope and freedom.**

HYMN OF PRAISE

CONFESSION

Leader: Let us join in our prayers of confession.

            Spirit of joy, with us always,
            through you, Christ lives in us, and we in Christ.
            Forgive us when we forget you
            and when we fail to live in your joy.
All: **Kyrie** *(sung – Taizé)*

Leader: Spirit of love, with us always.
            You bind us in love to yourself
            and to those around us.
            Forgive us when we hurt those we love
            and when we turn away
            from the love of our friends.

All:	**Kyrie** *(sung – Taizé)*
Leader:	Spirit of the Body of Christ, with us always, uniting us in the church with your life-giving grace and hope, Forgive us in our fragmenting of your church and our failure to carry your love into the world.
All:	**Kyrie** *(sung – Taizé)*
Leader:	Spirit in our world, with us always, comforting us, and drawing us into closer relationship with each other. Forgive us our wars and our hatreds, forgive our failure to recognise you, who lives in us all.
All:	**The Spirit is with us reconciling us to God.**

LIGHTING OF THE PENTECOST CANDLE

Reader 1:	The Spirit of faithfulness is the gift of the earth.

(A wick is lit.)

Reader 2:	The Spirit of imagination and variety comes to us from many countries.

(A wick is lit.)

Reader 3:	The Spirit of hope breathes in the poor and homeless in this city.

(A wick is lit.)

Reader 4:	The Spirit of freedom was announced by those who went before us and we proclaim it again today.

(A wick is lit.)

Leader:	The Spirit of love is Christ's gift to the church in every age.

(The centre flame is lit.)

People:	**We see the flame of the Spirit of God.**

(Candles are brought forward by representatives of various countries.)

Each representative: The Spirit is alive in... *(names country)*

People:	**We see the flame of the Spirit.**

Leader: The Spirit is
dancing
moving
struggling
rising
and calling to the ends of the earth.
We are forgiven and freed to new things.
People: **We have seen the flame of the Spirit**
in our midst.
Thanks be to God.

THE GLORIA

THE SERVICE OF THE WORD
Reader 1: Hear the word of God in the Old Testament.

(A reading from the Old Testament)

In this is the word of the Lord.
People: **Thanks be to God.**

THE PSALM   *(Sung)*
Reader 2: Hear the word of God in the Letters.

(A Reading from the New Testament Letters)

In this is the word of the Lord.
People: **Thanks be to God.**

HYMN OF FAITH

GOSPEL
Reader 3: Hear the word of God in the Gospel.

(After the reading)

In this is the word of the Lord.
People: **Thanks be to God.**

THE CONTEMPORARY WITNESS

AFFIRMATION OF FAITH
Leader: Let us stand and affirm our faith.
All: **We believe**
in God the creator
who gives birth to all that is
with labour and sighing
and looks to the world with joy and love.

We believe
in Christ the reconciler,
who is earthed in our life
and enfleshed in its patterns of dying and rising,
who gives honour to our reality
and grace to our way.

We believe
in God the free Spirit,
who weeps with our grievings
in the depths of our darkness
and dances among us high on life's mountains –
the Spirit who finds us with newness and hope.

We believe
in the community of faith,
which is born of our humanness,
is nurtured in sharing
and grows whole in our struggling
and celebration
as one people of God.

INTERCESSION

Leader: Let us join in prayer
            for the work of the Spirit around the world.

(The people bring their prayers for different countries.)

After each prayer the response:

All: Lord, Lord, hear us.

Leader: Spirit of justice,
            Spirit of peace,
            Spirit of Christ,
            our comforter, advocate and guide,
            we pray for your church:
People: May we ever reflect your life
            and your love.
            May we ever give power to
            your light and the passionate
            energy of your renewing spirit.
            Amen.

SERVICE OF THE EUCHARIST

THE OFFERING
Leader: Let us bring our offerings to God.

(The offering is received.)

THE SETTING OF THE TABLE
Leader: This table stands among us –
Christ's table
and our table.

People: **We gather around it
in our common humanness,
one people in our frailty,
none more worthy than the other;
all made worthy
in the resurrection of Christ
and the power of the Spirit.**

Leader: Little children stand under it.
Old people hold onto it.
Symbols of our life are placed onto it.
With joy we dress it in colour and light

People: **With joy we bring our gifts.
In faith we name it
our Holy table
as it carries the Body of Christ.**

*(The bread, the wine and the offerings of the people
are placed on the table.)*

THE GREAT THANKSGIVING
Leader: The Lord be with you
People: **And also with you**

Leader: Lift up your hearts
People: **We lift them to the Lord**

Leader: Let us give thanks to the Lord our God.
People: **It is right to give our thanks and praise.**

Leader: Creator God,
thank you
for the moving of the rock,
the dancing of life,
the running of the water,
the rising of the trees
and the birth of humankind.

People: **Thank you**
            for the coming of Jesus Christ our Saviour;
            for his life of joyful loving,
            his dying
            and his rising splendid.

Leader: Thank you
            for the gift of the Spirit,
            the flame of truth,
            the wind of freedom,
            the song of hope in every age.

People: **With those who have gone before us**
            and those who will come after us,
            we worship you
            in songs of never-ending praise:

All: **'Santo, santo, santo'** *(sung twice – WCC)*

THE INSTITUTION

INVOCATION OF THE HOLY SPIRIT

MEMORIAL PRAYER

THE LORD'S PRAYER

THE PEACE
Leader: The peace of the Lord be always with you.
People: **And also with you.**

THE BREAKING OF THE BREAD

THE DISTRIBUTION

FINAL THANKSGIVING

COMMISSIONING HYMN

BLESSING
Leader: Go in peace.
            And may God be in your creating,
            Christ be found in your midst,
            and the Spirit lead you to life.
            Amen.
All: **Amen.**

THREEFOLD AMEN *(AHB/WOV, No. 579)*

LITURGY FOR TRINITY SUNDAY

THE PREPARATION
Leader: Let us worship God.

PROCESSIONAL HYMN

CALL TO WORSHIP
Leader: God beyond all names and images,
People: **we worship you in faith.**

Leader: God in Christ with human face,
People: **we worship you in truth**

Leader: God who moves, draws, forms
            and enlightens our life,
People: **we worship you in Spirit.**
            God in three persons,
            God the beginning and God the end,
            you are our God.

HYMN OF PRAISE

CONFESSION
Leader: Let us join in our prayers of confession.

            God, we weep for the suffering of the world.
People: **Grant us peace.**

Leader: God, we weep for the suffering of the world.
People: **Grant us justice.**

Leader: God, we weep for our half-heartedness
               and weariness.
            God, we weep for our self-righteousness
               and indifference.
            God we weep for our silence and self-importance.
People: **Christ, have mercy upon us.**

Leader: Lord God, we weep for our guilt and powerlessness.
People: **Lord, have mercy upon us.**
Christ, have mercy upon us.
In your name, grant us peace.

ASSURANCE OF FORGIVENESS AND LOVE

Leader: Hear the Word in Christ:
happy are you who are poor:
yours is the kingdom of God.
Happy are you who are hungry now:
you shall be satisfied.
Happy are you who weep now:
you shall laugh.

Let us celebrate our struggling.
It is the pain of the birth
of the Word within us.
I pronounce us free and forgiven
in the name of Christ.
God be praised!
People: **Thanks be to God!**
All power and honour and glory
and praise to God.

THE SERVICE OF THE WORD

(A reading from the Old Testament)

Reader 1: This is the Word of the Lord.
People: **Thanks be to God.**

(A reading from the New Testament Letters)

Reader 2: This is the Word of the Lord.
People: **Thanks be to God.**

SENDING OUT OF THE CHILDREN

Leader: During the hymn of faith the children go out to
their program.

(The children are invited to gather at the front.)

We send you out as loved children of God.
Go in peace to learn and play together.
Amen.
People: **Amen.**

HYMN OF FAITH

GOSPEL

Leader: This is the Word of the Lord.
People: **Thanks be to God.**

THE CONTEMPORARY WITNESS

AFFIRMATION OF FAITH

Leader: Let us stand and affirm our faith.
All: Holy God,
dwelling in spaces
beyond the boundaries of our existence
and deep within us,
source of all light and life and author of love,
we believe in you.

Gracious God,
creating still, in the face of our nothingness
and always moving towards us
in loving relationship,
we believe in you.

Jesus Christ,
Son of God,
living in our midst,
restoring to us the beauty of our humanness,
entering every reality of our experience,
we believe in you.

Christ Jesus,
bearer of the pain of all our deaths,
true sign of the eternal victory of life,
one with us and one with God,
in ultimate reconciliation,
we believe in you.

Holy Spirit,
moving power like breath of wind through life,
enabling, recreating, interpreting,
ever pointing to newness and hope,
we believe in you.

Holy Spirit,
who through your being brings us to God
and brings us to Christ,

who gathers up our history
and firmly places it in the hope of the kingdom,
we believe in you.

God in three revelations,
God in all time,
God in all space,
we respond to you:
through the community of faith, the church,
in lives lived in the confidence of forgiveness,
and with the vision which flows
from our belief in the resurrection,
which is now,
and is yet to come.
Amen.

PRAYERS OF INTERCESSION

Leader: Let us join together in our prayers of intercession.

We hear your voice, O God,
saying 'Whom shall I send
and who will go for us?'
And we long to answer,
'Here I am. Send me'.

People: **Give us the faith to follow you, O God.**

Leader: We hear the cry of the powerless
and the suffering in the world
and know you are moving towards them,
Jesus Christ.

People: **Give us the faith to follow you, O Christ.**

Leader: We feel the loneliness, the fear
and the alienation around us in the city,
and we believe you are there,
comforting, encouraging and reconciling,
Holy Spirit.

People: **Give us the faith to follow you, O Spirit of God.**

Leader: We experience your life among us in your church,
calling us, confronting us, loving us
and giving us hope
as Creator, Redeemer and Life giver.

People: **Give us the faith to follow you, O God,
who is beyond our imagining.**

Leader:	And now let those who will
	lift up their particular prayers
	for the church and the world...

(The people offer their prayers.)

Leader:	Our God is with us:
People:	**In hope,**
	in community,
	in recreation
	and in leading us forth into the unknown.
	We are here, gracious God,
	send us.
	Amen.

THE OFFERING

| Leader: | Let us bring our offering before God. |

THE DEDICATION   *(All standing)*

Leader:	We are called to make real
	the sharing of the gifts God has given to us.
People:	**We offer what we have**
	for the good of all.
All:	**Amen.**

THE COMMISSIONING HYMN

BLESSING AND DISMISSAL

Leader:	We are the people who lived in darkness
	and have seen a great light.
People:	**Let us carry that light into the world.**

Leader:	God go with you as your creation,
	Christ go with you as your company,
	and may the Holy Spirit give you hope and peace.
	Amen.
People:	**Amen.**

THREEFOLD AMEN   *(AHB/WOV, No. 579)*

LITURGY FOR THE ENDING OF THE YEAR

Leader: Let us worship God.

PROCESSIONAL HYMN

CALL TO WORSHIP
Leader: God of all time,
            God of eternity,
People: **our years belong to you.**

Leader: Our endings
            are often your beginnings.
People: **Our dreamings
            are often your realities.**

Leader: Your affirm our past
People: **and give life to our future.
            We worship you.**

HYMN OF PRAISE

PRAYERS OF CONFESSION
Leader: Let us bring before God
            our prayers of confession.

            Shine the light of your truth upon us, O God,
            that we may see more clearly
            who we have been and who we are.

                        (Silence)

            Sometimes we have not been prepared
                to commit ourselves
            to the hope to which you have called us.
            And sometimes we have failed
            to do what we set out to do.
People: **Forgive us, O God, and call us again to new life.**
Leader: We look at our church and our world
            and still we see the injustices,
            the conflict and the suffering.

People: **Forgive us, O God, and call us again to new life.**

ASSURANCE OF PARDON
Leader: The gospel in Jesus Christ
            is that we may celebrate the year that is past
            and prepare to enter the new year without guilt.
            A new day is ours and we may claim it
            with hope and courage.
            Amen.
All: **Amen.**

THE MINISTRY OF THE WORD
Reader 1:   Hear the Word of God in the Old Testament.

            (A reading from the Old Testament)

            This is the Word of God.
People: **Thanks be to God.**

Reader 2:   Hear the Word of God in the Letters.

            (A reading from the New Testament Letters)

            This is the Word of the Lord.
People: **Thanks be to God.**

HYMN OF FAITH
Witness: Hear the Word of God in the Gospel.

            (A reading from the Gospel)

            This is the Word of the Lord.
People: **Thanks be to God.**

THE CONTEMPORARY WITNESS

THE AFFIRMATION OF FAITH
Leader: In response to the Word,
            let us stand and affirm our faith.

All: **The creativity of God
            fills the universe.
            Like rain falling upon the earth
            and sun warming the rocks,
            the heart of God
            flows over us all
            in renewing grace and love.**

The generosity of Christ
fills our lives.
With company on the journey
and mercy in understanding,
the Bread, the Way
and the Truth
set us free to live again.

The faithfulness of the Spirit
fills our future.
It surrounds us with a cloud of hope
and lifts our tired feet once more.
In courage born
of costly life,
it calls and sings
and dances on.

We are the people of freedom.
We lay down our past
in God's forgiveness.
We will walk on
into God's new day.

PRAYER OF THANKSGIVING AND INTERCESSION

Leader: Let us pray.
         You have called us by name
         and we belong to you, gracious God.
People: **When we passed through deep waters,**
         you have been with us.

Leader: When we walked through rivers,
         we have not been swept away.
People: **Above us**
         you have been
         the pillar of cloud by day
         and the pillar of flame by night.

Leader: As we travel to the end of the year
         we are thankful
         that you have been our company,
         and our light.
People: **But we do not travel alone,**
         O God.

> We bring you our prayers
> for our life
> and the life of the world.

Leader: In the face of wars and rumours of wars:
People: **we pray for peace.**

Leader: In the midst of racism and sexism:
People: **we pray for reconciliation and unity.**

Leader: As we look at poverty, oppression and exploitation:
People: **we pray for justice, for freedom**
and an end to human greed.

Leader: In a society where there is loneliness, pain and grief:
People: **we pray for true community**
where people care for and comfort each other.

Leader: As a church which stands among your divided
church:
People: **we pray that we will be one,**
that the world may believe you are love.
Leader: And now let those who will,
lift up their prayers for the church and the world...

(The people offer their prayers.)

Our hope is joined with yours, O God.

All: **Make us part of your healing,**
your mercy,
and the life of your Word
which has entered the world.
For we pray in faith.
Amen.

THE OFFERING
Leader: Let us bring our offerings before God.

THE DEDICATION *(All standing)*
Leader: Receive the offering of our gifts, O God.
People: **For we bring them with all that we are**
and all that we have been in this year.
Amen.

THE COMMISSIONING

THE COMMISSIONING HYMN

THE DISMISSAL

Leader: As Joseph and Mary were called into Egypt,
be prepared to go forth into the world.

People: **We go in faith.**
We go in hopefulness.

Leader: And may God the creator give you life,
God the heart of unity grant you community,
and God the healer and reconciler give you a love
which makes all things new.
Amen.

People: **Amen.**

THREEFOLD AMEN   *(AHB/WOV, No. 579)*

Services on themes and issues

"We believe in God
whose breath
brings the gift of life;
whose creativity
makes newness out of nothing;
whose love
sends us the Christ."

TAIZÉ HEALING SERVICE

INTRODUCTION

When entering a healing service, the congregation needs a clear understanding of its own theology of healing so that it can proceed with confidence.

We say:

When we pray for healing, we pray with confidence and expect to receive a response from a loving God. We are not God. Therefore, although we ask for healing as though we are speaking to a loving parent, we cannot determine the answer. When we pray, we believe that we bring together all our love, healing and energy with the powerful healing love and energy of God. We wait with faith and expectancy for the gifts to be given.

GREETING

Leader: The Lord be with you.
People: **And also with you.**

Leader: Let us worship God.

PROCESSIONAL HYMN

THE APPROACH

Leader: O God, you brought forth light out of darkness
            and out of nothing you created the universe.
People: **With uncertainty and fear**
            we come into the mystery of your presence.

Leader: O Christ, you lived among us;
            you taught and healed us
            and showed your great love
            by embracing the bitter cross.
People: **With longing and hope**
            we come into the mystery of your presence.

Leader: O Holy Spirit,
            you come to us in the rushing wind and fire,
            bringing strength and comforting and healing.
People: **With open hearts and minds**
            we come into the mystery of your presence.

All: We praise you, loving God.
        Be in our midst today,
        bringing light, love and strength.
        Amen.

THE GLORIA *(sung – Taizé)*

CONFESSION
Reading – 2 Samuel 12:1-14

Leader: There was a time – there are some today, who
           believe that God would kill a child for the sin of its
           father or mother.
People: **Kyrie, Kyrie, eleison** *(sung – Taizé)*

Leader: There was a time – when they believed that God
           sent war to punish one guilty person by killing and
           maiming thousands. Some still believe this.
People: **Kyrie, Kyrie, eleison** *(sung – Taizé)*

Leader: There was a time – there are some of us, sometimes,
           who believe God needs pursuading to be merciful.
People: **Kyrie, Kyrie, eleison** *(sung – Taizé)*

Leader: There was a time – many of us on a bad day believe
           that God sends famine and sickness and misfortune
           to those who would rouse her anger.
People: **Kyrie, Kyrie, eleison** *(sung – Taizé)*

Leader: There was a time – not so long ago, when we
           believed that healing was a sort of lottery: some are
           lucky, some are not, according to God's whim.
People: **Kyrie, Kyrie, eleison** *(sung – Taizé)*

Leader: There are times – for all of us, when God appears
           absent, asleep, indifferent, dead.
People: **Kyrie, Kyrie, eleison** *(sung – Taizé)*
                        (silence)

CHANT: 'By night we travel in darkness' *(Taizé)*

ASSURANCE OF PARDON
Leader: The faithfulness of God is greater than our doubt.
           The innocence of Christ is stronger than our guilt.
           The Spirit of love surrounds us here and now,
           to make us whole.

SENDING OUT OF THE CHILDREN

THE LIGHTING OF CANDLES

(People are invited to come forward and join the children to light a candle, or wash their hands in the font.)

CHANT: 'Bless the Lord, my soul' *(Taizé)*

GOSPEL

THE CONTEMPORARY WITNESS

AFFIRMATION OF FAITH *(seated)*

All: We believe in God
          whose breath
          brings the gift of life;
          whose creativity
          makes newness out of nothing;
          whose love
          sent us the Christ;
          whose solidarity
          accompanies our deaths;
          whose power
          frees us to the resurrection;
          whose Spirit
          liberates us from powerlessness;
          whose grace
          stands under all our being;
          whose unity
          calls us to be the church
          and to live out the hope
          of the kingdom.

THE LORD'S PRAYER *(sung)*

LORD'S PRAYER

SILENT PRAYER

SERVICE OF HEALING

CHANT : 'Come, O Holy Spirit' *(Taizé)*

(During the chant, people are invited to come to the centre of the church to share in and receive the laying on of hands.)

People: **Come, O Holy Spirit** *(repeat – Taizé)*

PRAYER FOR HEALING
Spirit of God,
enter the life of this your loved child.
Come with your healing, your peace and your freedom.
We claim now your transforming power and love.

(This may be repeated as often as necessary for all who wish to receive the laying on of hands.)

INTERCESSIONS
Prayer of St Francis *(sung)*

All: **Make me a channel of your peace** *(SA, No. 66)*

(You are invited to light a candle for particular people or situations and if you wish, share your prayer with the congregation.)

CHANT *(softly)* 'O Christe, Domine Jesu' *(Taizé)*

OFFERING
Leader: Let us bring our offering before God.

(As the offering is received the choir will sing.)

PRAYER OF DEDICATION *(stand)*

Leader: Receive these our gifts, O God.
People: **We bring them to share with the world
            your grace and love.**

COMMISSIONING HYMN: 'Love is come again' *(ATN)*

BENEDICTION
Leader: Go forth into the world to take up your tasks.
            And may God's presence enlighten your way,
            Christ's love surround you,
            and the Holy Spirit be your strength.
            Amen.

CHANT: 'My peace I leave you, my peace I give you' *(Taizé)*
(As we sing the final chant you are invited to extinguish a candle.)

CHERISH THE EARTH

Leader: Let us hear God's call to cherish the earth.

PROCESSIONAL HYMN

CALL TO WORSHIP

Leader: Let us dream of our world
            where the species are infinite
People: **and our dreams will be delicate.**

Leader: Let us sing in a world
            with all voices in harmony
People: **and our song will be delicate.**

Leader: Let us walk in our world
            of warm light and fragility
People: **and our tread will be delicate.**

Leader: Let us go gently into a delicate world.
People: **Let us worship God.**

HYMN OF PRAISE

PRAYERS OF CONFESSION

Leader: Creator God, you have showered us with gifts
                of great delicacy and delight:
                spider's web and butterfly's wings,
                roaring seas and majestic forests.
            Let us remember in reverence your presence
                in all creation.

                (Silence)

Leader: O God, your creation fills us with awe and delight,
            yet we often fail to care for its creatures.
People: **Forgive, us gracious God,**
            and create in us a new way of caring.

Leader: We witness the destruction of many species
                through pollution and carelessness.
            We are often the careless ones,
                and slow to work for change.

131

People:	**Forgive us, gracious God,** **and spur us to act for change.**
Leader:	In the land of Dreaming and Aboriginal wisdom, we have often been slow to listen, preferring the 'white' way of progress, exploitation and greed.
People:	**Forgive us, gracious God,** **and give us the wisdom to listen and learn.**
All:	**Open all our senses, O God,** **to the miracles around us.**

ASSURANCE OF PARDON

Leader:	Our God is just and forgiving. Our God warns us and calls us to change before it is too late. Our God receives us as we are; lifts us up and appoints us again to care for the earth and all its creatures. Receive the grace of God in all its strength and delicate beauty. The old order has passed away and the new creation is before us.
People:	**Thanks be to God.**

MINISTRY OF THE WORD

Reader 1:	Hear the Word of God in the Old Testament.
	(A reading from the Old Testament)
	This is the Word of the Lord.
People:	**Thanks be to God.**
Reader 2:	Hear the Word of God in the Letters.
	(A reading from the New Testament Letters)
	This is the Word of the Lord.
People:	**Thanks be to God.**

SENDING OUT OF THE CHILDREN

Poem: 'The Tree'
(by the children of Pitt Street Uniting Church)

Leader:	Sheltering
	huge, spreading, twisting
People:	**Part of God's creation.**

Leader:	Death, chopping
	to keep in touch
	to write words on paper
	to learn
People:	**Part of God's creation.**

Leader:	Observer, provider
	part of the food chain
	the forest
People:	**Part of God's creation**

Leader:	Pleasure, comfort
	furniture in homes
	the warmth of fire
People:	**Part of God's creation.**

Leader:	We send you out as loved children of God.
	Go in peace to learn and play together.
	Amen.
People:	**Amen.**

HYMN OF FAITH
Witness: Hear the word of God in the Gospel.

(A reading from the Gospel)

This is the Word of the Lord.
People: **Thanks be to God.**

THE CONTEMPORARY WITNESS

AFFIRMATION OF FAITH
Leader: In response to the Word,
let us stand and affirm our faith.

All: **We believe in God,**
who is found in darkness,
who parted the waters with a dream,
fragrant as the ancient damask rose;
who made from nothing – light,
stars, moons, planets and loveliest earth;
who ran wild with joy, creating

mountains, waves and snowflakes.
All different...

Who spun a web of shimmering life
where creatures grew and changed,
flowered and put down roots,
swam,
chirped and flew,
ran, played and roared,
talked – in many different languages –
wondered and dreamed
beings of astonishing variety,
each needing all the others,
held in a delicate kinship.

God saw that it was very good
and laughed and made some more.

We believe in God
who is found in waiting,
who patiently provides for each
according to their need,
who blankets the drowsy wintering spider
with warm earth
so she may go about her business in the
     springtime,
feared and respected by her neighbours.

We believe in God
who is found in stillness,
who walks in the world, awake and vulnerable,
delighting and loving,
bright as wattle in the sunshine,
who grieves in the quiet beyond tears
for scorched wilderness,
     stifled air
     wounded forests
     silenced voices
     broken threads –
who names the truth
and shoulders the weight of hoping.

We believe in God
who is found in loneliness,
who speaks in the dawn birdsong

the grieving call of whales
the music of stars.

We believe God calls us as the church
to love the earth,
to live humbly in the web of relationship,
to announce the new wilderness.

PRAYERS OF INTERCESSION AND THANKSGIVING

Leader: Creator God, who spoke,
brought forth and it was good,
who holds this now distorted world
still in your hands,
we remember that Christ has come
to make all things new.

As we see urban abuse around us,
we pray for a live conscience.

People: **May we create clean hearts in our cities, O God.**

Leader: As we hear of raped forests and stripped mountains,
we pray for an understanding
of the delicacy of nature.

People: **Put a new and right spirit in us
that we may restore and recover.**

Leader: As we experience global oil spills and pollution
and mourn marine-life lost and birds maimed,
we pray for enlightenment in our policies.

People: **Break down our angry destruction
that our beaches and rivers
may speak again of your wonders.**

Leader: As we touch the darkened lives of many people
who long for a bit of sun
in the battle for survival,
we pray for compassion
and generous giving of time.

People: **Open up our ears
that we may hear their cries of anguish.**

Leader: Mother-father God, whose beauty has not changed,
we also give thanks for the things in creation
that delight us.

(People are invited to name specific things.)

Leader: We give thanks for all these things that delight us.
All: **To you, God of creation,**
        we sing a new song of praise.
    A song of trees planted by streams of living water,
    a song of mountains clapping their hands for joy,
    a song of cities delighting in heavenly harmony,
    a song of people that were lost
        and have been found.
    For the earth is the Lord's
        and we shall be glad in it.
    Hallelujah. Amen.

THE OFFERING

Leader: Let us bring our offering to God.

(The offering is received.)

THE DEDICATION *(All standing)*

Leader: In response to the immeasurable wonder and
    diversity of God's creation, we bring these gifts.
People: **And dedicate them to sustaining**
        the fragile web of all life on earth.
All: **Amen.**

THE COMMISSIONING

THE COMMISSIONING HYMN

THE SENDING OUT AND BLESSING

Leader: Go out to care for God's earth
    in all its varied and fragile beauty.
People: **We go out with trust and courage**
    to care for the earth,
        our home and our children' home.

Leader: May God the Creator restore our hope and vision.
    May the Christ who walked the earth go with us.
    And may the Holy Spirit empower us
    to see the pattern of the universe.
    Amen.
People: **Amen.**

THREEFOLD AMEN *(AHB/WOV, No. 579)*

A CELEBRATION OF THE FAMILY

GREETING

Leader: We are all part of the rhythm of life:
we are born,
we give birth,
we live in relationships,
we search for meaning,
we make choices,
we die,
we suffer the loss of those we love.
As we celebrate this day of the journey,
peace be with you,

People: **and also with you.**

PROCESSIONAL HYMN

CALL TO WORSHIP

Leader: In your image we are made, Creator God,
People: **male and female, young and old,**
we are your creation.

Leader: You took on our life, Jesus Christ.
People: **We find you there**
in truth and grace within ourselves.

Leader: You lead us, on Holy Spirit,
People: **in golden threads of life**
in pain and joy.
Thanks be to God!

HYMN OF PRAISE

CONFESSION

Leader: We had a dream about families, O God.
It looked like many lights
from a great stream of people
generation after generation,
adding to each other's light,
warming each other's life
setting each other free

across the boundaries
of all our differences,
creating in between
the brave and gracious light
of human community.

(The candle is lit.)

(Silent reflection)

Leader: We are remembering
how far we are from that dream.

(Silent reflection)

Leader: O God, so often it is the small
things that defeat us:
the lid off the toothpaste,
the bathmat in a heap,
one more unwiped bench,
the last grizzle from somebody,
another gift taken for granted.
These small things build upon each other, God,
and when our energy is low
and our hurts are high,
they take from our life.
It is often hard to live as families.
Lord, have mercy

All: **Lord, have mercy** *(SA, No 99a)*

ASSURANCE OF PARDON

Leader: Hear the word of grace in Jesus Christ:
the love of God for us never fails.
Nothing can separate us from that love.
A new dream is always ours.
Rise up and live in freedom and faith.
Amen.

People: **Amen.**

THE GLORIA

THE MINISTRY OF THE WORD

Reader 1:   Hear the Word of God in the Old Testament.

(A reading from the Old Testament)

In this is the Word of the Lord.

People: **Thanks be to God.**

Reader 2:   Hear the Word of God in the Letters.

(A reading from the New Testament Letters)

In this is the Word of the Lord.
People: **Thanks be to God.**

SENDING OUT OF THE CHILDREN

(The children gather at the front.)

Leader: We send you out to learn
that God loves the world
and all its people,
and that God loves you.
Amen.
People: **Amen.**

HYMN OF FAITH

Witness: Hear the Word of God in the Gospel.

(A reading from the Gospel)

This is the Gospel of the Lord.
People: **Praise to you, Lord Jesus Christ.**

THE CONTEMPORARY WITNESS

AFFIRMATION OF FAITH

Leader: In response to the Word, let us
stand and affirm our faith:

All: **Birth comes through membranes of pain.
In the fragile claiming of life,
the drawing in of breath,
we are with God,
creator of heaven and earth,
maker of all that is.**

**Life comes through walking on,
and in the entering of death,
the daring to face our truths,
we are with Christ,
who died and lived with us,
who defeated death.**

**And in each moment of the way,
in lifting heart and freedom won,
in dreams untold and hopes of love,**

the Spirit calls us on
with songs of life
and glimpses of community.

We are the church,
a family of faith.
Within this frail body,
we live in peace.

PRAYERS OF INTERCESSION

Leader: In our homes, we are family,
in the church, we are family,
in the community, we are family,
in the whole creation, we are family.
In every place, we depend on you, O God.
In faith we pray for the moments
in our life when we need your help.

(The people offer their prayers.)

Response after each petition:
People: **We pray for this moment in our life.**

Leader: All these prayers,
and the silent prayers within our hearts,
we offer to you, O God of grace.
Show us the liberating love
which you give to us
that we may free each other
for life
and trustingly place in your hands
those who leave us in death.
O Lord, hear our prayer.

All: *(sung)* **O Lord, hear our prayer,**
O Lord, hear our prayer,
When we call answer us.
O Lord, hear our prayer,
Come and listen to us. *(Taizé)*

SERVICE OF THE EUCHARIST

THE OFFERING

Leader: Let us bring our offerings before God.

(The offering is received.)

DEDICATION *(all standing)*

GREAT PRAYER OF THANKSGIVING

THE LORD'S PRAYER

THE BREAKING OF THE BREAD

THE DISTRIBUTION

PASSING OF THE PEACE

PRAYER AFTER COMMUNION

COMMISSIONING HYMN

BLESSING
Leader: God go with you into this day,
             Christ Jesus walk before you,
             and the Spirit be a cloud of grace.

THE RIGHTS OF THE CHILD

GREETING

Leader: Grace and peace to you
in the name of Creator,
Christ and Holy Spirit.

People: **May grace and peace
be yours also.**

PROCESSIONAL HYMN

THE APPROACH

Leader: Become as little children
and you will come closer to God.

People: **For God honours the humble
and vulnerable in life.**

Leader: Become as little children
and you will understand trust.

People: **For God receives with joy
the childlike openness to love.**

CELEBRATION OF THE VALUES OF CHILDREN

Leader: Some of our children will share with us
things about their life which they value.

(Presentation by the children.)

PRAYERS OF CONFESSION

Leader: Dear God,
of your kindness you give us children
for fun, and for hope.
But often we fail our children
and lose our dream.

All: **Kyrie** *(sung – Taizé)*

Leader: We all say children have the right
to peace and love,
but in our violent world
even children are tortured and killed.
They suffer the terror of war
with no-one to comfort them.

All:	**Kyrie** *(sung – Taizé)*
Leader:	We say children have the right to a name and a nationality, but many children live for years in the half-life of refugee camps, waiting to belong to someone.
All:	**Kyrie** *(sung – Taizé)*
Leader:	We say children have the right to adequate nutrition and medical care, but some get far too much while many die, or survive damaged by malnutrition and disease.
All:	**Kyrie** *(sung – Taizé)*
Leader:	We say disabled children have the right to special care, but this is often provided in ways that keep them dependent and their gifts are unrecognised.
All:	**Kyrie** *(sung – Taizé)*
Leader:	We say children have the right to the love and care of their family, but sometimes parents are too hurt to love and too tired to care.
All:	**Kyrie** *(sung – Taizé)*

ASSURANCE OF PARDON

Leader:	Hear the good news. Through God who knows us from the beginning, we are named, we are loved as children of God. Through Christ who came as a child, our children are given back to us. We are free to play, to grow, to make mistakes, to learn with them the dance of life. Amen.
All:	**Amen.**

Leader: Let us stand and sing:

HYMN OR SONG OF PRAISE

THE MINISTRY OF THE WORD
Reader 1:   Hear the Word of God in the Old Testament.

(A reading from the Old Testament)

This is the Word of the Lord.
People: **Thanks be to God.**

Reader 2:   Hear the Word of God in the Letters.

(A reading from the New Testament Letters)

This is the Word of the Lord.
People: **Thanks be to God.**

SENDING OUT OF THE CHILDREN

(If children are to be sent to a program use this.)

Leader: We send you to your program to learn that
            God is always with you and that we love you.
            Amen.
People: **Amen.**

HYMN OF FAITH
Witness: Hear the Word of God in the Gospel.

(A reading from the Gospel)

This is the Word of the Lord.
People: **Thanks be to God.**

THE CONTEMPORARY WITNESS

AFFIRMATION OF FAITH
Leader: Let us say what we believe.

People: **We believe in God**
            who was there
            at the secret, quiet moments of conception,
            when the 'self' that is in each of us was created,
            and a thousand other possibilities turned away.

            We believe in God
            who sang a murmuring song to us
            in the nurturing closeness of the womb;

who watched with joy
as we grew and moved and became strong
and aware and ready for birth.

We believe in God
who called us on that first great journey
into light,
who breathed into us the breath of life;
who speaks to us through our parents,
our children, our friends, our enemies.

We believe in God
who does not leave us
even in our darkness
when we have lost the way home.
God calls us again and again
to new adventures,
new stairs to climb,
new questions to ask,
new people to love.

Our God is in bread and sunshine,
and parties,
and most beautifully in our children.

PRAYERS OF INTERCESSION

(The children may come to stand by the table.)

Leader: Loving God,
we thank you for our children.
And we pray that children everywhere
will be made welcome,
fed and cared for,
protected from harm,
affirmed in being.
We ask that there may be wilderness
for them to play in,
and children of many races to be their friends,
so they may grow in grace
and dream your dreams
and learn the ways of your creation.

We ask this for the children of this parish...

All: **Jesus, remember them...** *(sung – Taizé)*

Leader: The children of Australia...
All: **Jesus, remember them...** *(sung – Taizé)*

Leader: The children of the world...

(Children and/or adults might name countries here.)

Leader: Jesus, remember them.

(Children return to their seats during singing of this chant.)

All: **Jesus, remember them...** *(sung – Taizé)*

Leader: We remember before you
the people who long for children –
whose children have gone away,
or are lost,
or do not know them.
Those whose children have died.
Those whose children were never conceived.

(Pause)

Leader: Jesus, remember them.
People: **Jesus, remember them...** *(sung – Taizé)*

THE OFFERING

Leader: Let us offer our gifts
as a sign of our commitment
to Christ and the world.

PRAYER OF DEDICATION *(All standing)*

Leader: Let us praise God.
People: **O God, who calls us from death to life,
we give ourselves to you
and with the church through all ages,
we thank you for your saving love
in Jesus Christ our Lord.
Amen.**

THE COMMISSIONING

HYMN

THE DISMISSAL AND BLESSING

Leader: Go in faith as children of God,
and may God, the loving parent,
take you by the hand,
God the Christ be your pathway,
and God the Spirit lead you to truth.
Amen.

All: **Amen.**

THREEFOLD AMEN   *(AHB/WOV, No. 579)*

CELEBRATION OF CREATION

GREETING
The whole universe is a gift of God.
Everything here is a gift of God.
We are the gifts of God to each other.
We are all part of the procession of life.
Let us stand and celebrate by joining together
in the procession around the aisles of the church
as we sing the processional hymn.

PROCESSIONAL HYMN

CALL TO WORSHIP
Leader: Out of nothingness we came
            through birth into life:
People: **With the Spirit of God within us.**

Leader: From the life of God
            the universe unfolded into being:
People: **With the Spirit of God within it.**

Leader: From the heart of God
            creation goes on till the end of time:
People: **With the Spirit of God within it
            and with our spirit within it.**

Leader: Let us embrace the God who enfolds us.
People: **We delight in God.**

HYMN OF PRAISE

CONFESSION
Leader: Let us bring to God our confession:

            Creator God,
            we confess that our creating often goes wrong.
            We are sometimes ignorant.
            We are sometimes careless.
            We are sometimes short-sighted
            and self-interested.
            Let us be aware of our failures in creation.

                    (Silence)

Let us name those things before God.

(The people contribute.)

Leader: Forgive us, gracious God.
People: **We long to live in harmony
with all that you have given to us.**

ASSURANCE OF PARDON

Leader: God is always the creator
and the recreator.
People: **Let us celebrate the recreation
which is offered to us at this moment!**

THE MINISTRY OF THE WORD

The witness of Scripture

Other witnesses

The children prepare their witness

HYMN OF FAITH

THE CONTEMPORARY WITNESS

A LITANY OF CREATION AND CREATING

Leader: Let us stand and affirm creation together.
People: **God spoke light into the void
and the light is in our hands
against the darkness.
God clothed the world with sky
and we ride upon the wind
and breathe among the leaves.
God gifted us with earth
and with water in between.
We dig and float
and drink and grow
and know the power of earth and sea.
We paint and sing and work and dance
in company with God.
We share the earth with all that is
in harmonies of warm and cold,
in green and desert,
crowd and lone,
we feel the pain,
we feel the joy.**

149

**God is our mother,
God is our father,
Christ is our brother,
the Spirit is within us.
We celebrate our sharing
in the recreating of the world.**

PRAYERS OF INTERCESSION

Leader: Let us sit still among the pain of the world.

(Silence)

Let us name it.

(Contributions from people)

Leader: Beside each other, within the earth,
we are in her and of her,
are vulnerable with her,
are her people.
We are the people of pain and fear,
we are the people of anger and joy,
we are the people of compassion and grace.

People: **We are each of us this,
we are all of us this,
we name our God,
we are one.**

Leader: In all of us is a longing
for a life that has not yet come,
for a world that is free and just,
a dream of hope for all people.

People: **Together with God
we will create that possibility.
Amen.**

THE OFFERING

Leader: Let us give as those who receive.

(The offering is received.)

THE DEDICATION   *(All standing)*

Leader: Receive these our gifts, gracious God.
People: **In hope and thanksgiving
we offer them to you.
Amen.**

THE COMMISSIONING

THE COMMISSIONING HYMN

THE BLESSING AND DISMISSAL

Leader: Go forth and share in
the recreating of the world.

People: **We go in faith
to be the people of the new creation.**

Leader: May the sun warm your soul
and the moon be gentle above you.
May the Creator hold your hand
and the Christ walk in your footsteps.
May the Spirit dance in your playing
and grace be found in your way.
Amen.

All: **Amen.**

THREEFOLD AMEN *(AHB/WOV, No. 579)*

LITURGY FOR
CHURCH UNION SUNDAY

Leader: Let us worship God.

PROCESSIONAL HYMN

CALL TO WORSHIP
Leader: Praise to God for the gifts of the past:
People: **for the witness of the people of God
            who went before us.**

Leader: Praise to God for the gifts of the present:
People: **in all our struggles to be true to the Christ.**

Leader: Praise to God for the gifts in our future:
People: **in the Spirit we are led on
            into crucifixions and resurrections.
            Amen.**

HYMN OF PRAISE

LIGHTING OF THE CANDLES
Leader: We light this candle for our heritage in the
            Congregational tradition with its commitment to
            freedom and to the power of the priesthood of all
            believers.

            (The candle is lit.)

People: **We will stand in that great tradition.**

Leader: We light this candle for our heritage in the
            Methodist tradition with its commitment to social
            justice and its enthusiasm in communicating the
            gospel.

            (The candle is lit.)

People: **We will stand in that great tradition.**

Leader: We light this candle for our heritage in the
            Presbyterian tradition with its respect for

scholarship and its deep understanding of the nature of the church.

(The candle is lit.)

People: **We will stand in that great tradition.**

Leader: We light this fourth candle to celebrate the other great traditions which are now joined with us in this parish including Catholic, Anglican, Orthodox, Baptist, Churches of Christ and Pentecostal in all their diversity and all their faith.

(The candle is lit.)

People: **We will stand in these great traditions too.**
In Christ we are one.
In Christ everything is made new.
Thanks be to God!

PRAYERS OF CONFESSION

Leader: Let us join in our prayers of confession.

On the day of union we committed ourselves to be one people in the Spirit of Christ:

People: **and we are still divided.**

Leader: To be a pilgrim people:
People: **but often we have refused to move and change.**

Leader: To use the gifts of all the people for the kingdom:
People: **but we refuse to call forth the gifts**
and offer them to you.

Leader: To be servants to the world:
People: **but we have turned away into our own concerns**
and closed our eyes to the pain of others.

All: **Forgive us, O God,**
and help us to renew our commitment
to live out the hope to which we are called.

ASSURANCE OF PARDON

Leader: In Christ
our hope is new every day
and there is no condemnation.
Rise up and live as free people of God.
Amen.

People: **Amen.**

All: **Our father in heaven,**
             hallowed be your name,
             your kingdom come,
             your will be done
                  on earth as in heaven.
             Give us today our daily bread.
             Forgive us our sins
                  as we forgive those who sin against us.
             Save us from the time of trial
                  and deliver us from evil.
             For the kingdom, the power, and the glory
             are yours
             now and forever. Amen.

THE MINISTRY OF THE WORD

Reader 1:   Hear the Word of God in the Old Testament.

             (A reading from the Old Testament)

             This is the Word of the Lord.
People: **Thanks be to God.**

Reader 2:   Hear the Word of God in the Letters.

             (A reading from the New Testament Letters)

             This is the Word of the Lord.
People: **Thanks be to God.**

HYMN OF FAITH

Witness: Hear the Word of God in the Gospel.

             (A reading from the Gospel)

             This is the Word of the Lord.
People: **Thanks be to God.**

THE CONTEMPORARY WITNESS

Leader: Let us stand and celebrate the family of faith.

APOSTLES' CREED

PRAYERS OF INTERCESSION

Leader: In the spirit of our beginnings
             as the Uniting Church in Australia
             let us join in our prayers of intercession.

	As a church set in South East Asia and
	the Pacific:
People:	**make us true neighbours**
	to those among whom we live, O God.

Leader:	In a country which has been richly blessed:
People:	**give us the courage to stand for justice,**
	an end to poverty and discrimination
	and the support of that which offers dignity
	to all people.

Leader:	As those born into freedom:
People:	**may we uphold human rights,**
	participate in the constant search for truth,
	live with integrity and with concern
	for the whole human race.

Leader: And now let those who will
lift up their prayers for the church and the world...

(People offer their prayers.)

O God, we pray that nothing in all the earth
will separate us from your love in Christ Jesus.

People: **May we live as though we belong to you**
and be a humble sign of hope in this place
where we make our witness.

All: **Amen.**

OFFERING
Leader: Let us bring our offerings before God.

(The offering is received.)

DEDICATION *(All standing)*
Leader: O God, we offer these gifts
and all that we are as your church.

People: **Use them and us**
for the continuing of your creation.
Amen.

COMMISSIONING HYMN

DISMISSAL AND BENEDICTION

Leader: We are the church,
              the mission of God is ours.

People: **We go in hope and love
              into the world.**

Leader: May God the heart of life
                be deep within us,
              God the Christ
                be present in our history,
              and God the Spirit
                give us power, truth and peace.
              Amen.

THREEFOLD AMEN   *(AHB/WOV, No. 579)*

*(The prayers in this liturgy are based on the Basis of Union and the
Statement to the Nation on the occasion of the First Assembly of the
Uniting Church in Australia.)*

NATIONAL ABORIGINES SUNDAY

Leader: Let us worship God.

PROCESSIONAL HYMN

CALL TO WORSHIP
Leader: Our God is the God of the deeps of the earth
People: **and of the highest heavens.**

Leader: We gather in this place
           which is our home for worship,
People: **and we have unity with those
           who meet their God in other places.**

All: **Thanks be to God who encompasses us all
           and stretches beyond all our boundaries
           of understanding.**

HYMN OF PRAISE

LIGHTING OF THE LAND RIGHTS CANDLE
Leader: We light these candles
           in honour of Aboriginal people
           who live with dignity and courage,
           and for the great hope of reconciliation and justice.

PRAYERS OF CONFESSION
Leader: In penitence and faith,
           let us bring before God our prayers of confession.

           O God, we have no words
           as we face who we are on this day.
           We have only silent grief and repentance.
                        (Silence)
           Our history confronts us.
           Our present reality is still built on injustice
           and lack of reconciliation.
People: **God, forgive us,
           for we know what we do**

**and we see what we have done.
Amen.**

ASSURANCE OF PARDON
Leader: The Word to us in Christ stands firm.
While we are yet sinners,
we are set free and called to live a new day.
Rise up and walk forward
in truth and in justice.
Amen.
People: **Amen.**

THE MINISTRY OF THE WORD
Reader 1: Hear the Word of God in the Old Testament.

(A reading from the Old Testament)

This is the Word of the Lord.
People: **Thanks be to God.**

Reader 2: Hear the Word of God in the Letters.

(A reading from the New Testament Letters)

This is the Word of the Lord.
People: **Thanks be to God.**

SENDING OUT OF THE CHILDREN
Leader: We send you out as our loved children.
Go and learn that it is good
to live in a country
with people of many races and cultures
and that God loves us all.
Amen.
People: **Amen.**

HYMN OF FAITH
Witness: Hear the Word of God in the Gospel.

(A reading from the Gospel)

This is the Word of the Lord.
People: **Thanks be to God.**

THE CONTEMPORARY WITNESS

AFFIRMATION OF FAITH

Leader: In response to the Word,
            let us stand and say what we believe.

People: **We believe in God**
            who brought us forth from the earth our mother,
            who supplies our needs with fruits from the earth,
            who walks with us upon the earth,
            who moves us to love the earth,
            One God.

            We believe in God
            in whom past, present and future
            make one time.

            We believe in God
            in whom the deep warm movement of the earth,
            the driving wind,
            and the cool flowing of stars
            make one dance.

            We believe in God
            in whom black, white, red, brown and yellow,
            friends and enemies,
            make one people.

            We believe in God
            through whom thunder, music and the
            secret whisper of the Spirit
            make one call.

            We believe in God
            through whom a little seed
            grows to a tall gumtree
            and the prayer of a child brings peace
            in our world.

PRAYERS OF THANKSGIVING AND INTERCESSION

Leader: Let us join in our prayers of thanksgiving
            and intercession.

            God of imagination and love,
            we thank you that we are not created the same,
            that you have given to us
            the exciting riches of our diversity.

People: **Thanks be to God for the gift**
          of peoples of different races
          and colours and cultures – to love,
          to care for, to share lives with.

Leader: God of justice and reconciliation,
          we thank you that you will not let us rest
          until we all enter into your abundant life,
          life which is full and free and gracious.

People: **Thanks be to God for the hope**
          that we may live for better things,
          for justice for Aboriginal people,
          for release from exploitation and greed.

Leader: God who listens,
          God who empowers and saves us,
          we pray for the struggle to end
          Aboriginal deaths in custody.

People: **Let justice be done, O God.**

Leader: For all children in this country
          to have the same chance for life and health.

People: **Let justice be done, O God.**

Leader: For an end to prejudice and discrimination
          in attitudes and services.

People: **Let justice be done, O God.**

Leader: For the bringing in of a new order
          where we live together in thankful harmony
          because we have rightly shared the land,
          paid our debts and recognised the dignity
          and worth of all people.

People: **Let justice be done, O God.**

Leader: Let those who will, lift up their prayers
          for the church and the world...

          (The people offer their prayers.)

          God, hear our prayers
          and make us part of your answer.
          Amen.

People: **Amen.**

THE OFFERING

Leader: Let us bring our gifts before God.

(The offering is received.)

PRAYER OF DEDICATION   *(All standing)*

Leader: All we have is yours, O God.

People: **Call us to give as freely as you have given to us and receive what we offer you. Amen.**

THE COMMISSIONING

COMMISSIONING HYMN

THE DISMISSAL

Leader: God has shown us what is good.

People: **What does the Lord require of us but to do justice to love kindness and to walk humbly with our God?**

Leader: Go forth into the world. May grace and peace be yours and your God go with you. Amen.

THREEFOLD AMEN   *(AHB/WOV, No. 579)*

Brief acts of worship

"May God go with us into this future;
Christ Jesus walk before us;
and the Spirit be a cloud of grace."

WORSHIP TO OPEN A MEETING

GREETING

Leader: Peace be with you.
People: **And also with you.**

CALL TO WORSHIP

Leader: O God, you are the gathering one
           who calls us into community
           with each other;
People: **to love and work,
           to support and heal.**

Leader: You are the gathering one
           who calls us into community
           with all people;
People: **to bring justice and hope,
           freedom and truth.**

Leader   You are the gathering one
           who calls us into community
           with the whole creation;
People: **to live in harmony,
           to cherish and renew.
           Let us worship the God
           who makes us one.**

SONG

CONFESSION

Leader: Let us remember who we are
           before the holiness of God.

                    (Silent reflection)

           O God, we have not yet
           lived in your life.
People: **We grieve the times
           when we have lost the way.
           Forgive us, O God of grace.**

ASSURANCE OF PARDON

Leader: Hear the words of assurance:
Christ has found us again
and claimed us as the children of God.
Lift up your heads and live!
Amen.

People: **Amen.**

MINISTRY OF THE WORD

PRAYERS OF INTERCESSION

Leader: O God, as we meet,
we are aware of the pain of the world
in the places we now name...

(The people name their particular concerns.)

In these situations and others
we have not named,
we need you, God.

People: **For we are not enough to save the world.**

Leader: We bring before you the church
with all its struggles to be true to the gospel.

(Silent prayer)

Leader: As we falter,
People: **lift us up.**

Leader: Where we are confused,
People: **give us wisdom.**

Leader: When we are tired and hurt,
People: **give us energy and healing.**

Leader: If we are afraid,
People: **give us the courage of your Spirit.**

Leader: And now we lay our task before you.
People: **Breathe into us the new life that we need.**
Open our hearts and minds
to the gifts of each other.
Surround us with the mystery of your love
and send us into your way.
Amen.

SONG

BLESSING

Leader: May God go with us into this future;
           Christ Jesus walk before us;
           and the Spirit be a cloud of grace.
           Amen.
People: **Amen.**

WORSHIP TO OPEN A MEETING IN THE EVENING

CALL TO WORSHIP *(All standing)*

Leader: We have come from the work of the day:

People: **and we are open to this moment together.**

Leader: We have left the place where we live:

People: **and we are gathered as the children of God.**

Leader: We have brought with us
the realities of our life:

People: **we wait with expectation
for the new realities in Christ.
Let us worship God.**

SONG

CONFESSION *(Seated)*

Leader: Let us bring our confessions before God.

O God,
you have given us the vision
of working for your kingdom,
but we fall far short of that hope.

People: **Forgive us, O God.**

Leader: You call us to be the Body of Christ,
but we fail to see the gifts
that are among us
and often stand divided.

People: **Forgive us, O God,
and give us faith, hope and love.
Amen.**

ASSURANCE OF PARDON

Leader: Hear the Word of God in Jesus Christ.

There is no condemnation for those who believe.
Rise up and live in freedom and faith.
Amen.

People: **Amen.**

THE BIBLE CONVERSATION

PRAYERS OF INTERCESSION

Leader: Let us pray our prayers of intercession.
People: **Lord of the whole creation,**
            we pray for the healing of the world.
            Bring peace and justice
            to all who suffer oppression
            and all who live in need.

Leader: Let us pray for this city.
People: **Christ who lives in our midst,**
            we pray for the city in which we are set.
            Bring life to its people
            and a true sense of community.
            Lift up your church
            as a sign of hope and love
            which points to the presence of God among us.

Leader: And now let those who will
            lift up their prayers
            for the church and the world...

                  (People pray for their concerns.)

Leader: Hear these our prayers,
            O gracious God,
            and give us courage, wisdom
            and the inspiration of your Holy Spirit
            in our work together now.
            Amen.
People: **Amen.**

BLESSING *(Standing)*

Leader: Take up the task
            which we have been given.
People: **We go forward in faith**
            because God is with us.

All: **Amen.**

EVENING WORSHIP

GREETING
Leader: The peace of God be with you all.
People: **And also with you.**

OPENING SENTENCES
Leader: The transforming winds of creative life
People: **are but the breath of God.**

Leader: The passionate flames of justice and love
People: **are the graceful signs of the Christ.**

Leader: The flights of freedom in movements of truth
People: **are the joyful life of the Spirit.**

All: **We celebrate this day
and the signs of God in our midst.**

HYMN

CONFESSION
Leader: Let us remember who we are
before the holiness of God.
All: **'Santo Santo Santo'**

(Sung twice – once in Spanish, once in English – WCC)

(Silent reflection)

Leader: Let us pray.
All: **Holy God,
we have failed to live in full
the generosity of your grace,
the costliness of your love
and the liberation of your free spirit.
Forgive us, and lead us into life.
Amen.**

ASSURANCE OF PARDON
Leader: Nothing can separate us
from the love of God in Christ Jesus.
In faith,

lay down the burden of this day
and enter the night in peace.
Amen.

People: **Amen.**

THE WORD

(A reading from the Bible)

(Silent reflection)

Leader: This is the word of the Lord.
People: **Thanks be to God.**

PRAYERS OF INTERCESSION

Leader: Come, Holy Spirit, renew the whole creation.
            Move in our labouring
            with the energy of your being
            and bring to birth in us
            the renewal of your church.
People: **Come, Holy Spirit,**
            renew the whole creation.

Leader: Move in the world
            with the streams of your justice.
            Give waters of life to the poor
            and rivers of freedom to the oppressed.
People: **Come, Holy Spirit,**
            renew the whole creation.

Leader: Move in our hearts
            with the fire of your love.
            Spread the warmth of your healing
            and the flame of your transforming power.
People: **Come, Holy Spirit,**
            renew the whole creation.
            In the name of Christ.
            Amen.

SONG: 'You are holy' *(WCC)*

LITANY FOR THE NIGHT

Leader: The night is the cover of your peace, O God,
People: **the rhythm of your rest for all your people.**

Leader:	The darkness is the cloak of your gentleness, O God,
People:	**the warmth of your hand around the earth.**
Leader:	In its blackness, is the sign of your eternity,
People:	**the never-ending living of your love.**
Leader:	In faith we go to sleep and leave our life to you.
People:	**In child-like trust we end our efforts of this day. In our sleeping, be our company. In our waking, be the gift of our new day.**
Leader:	Go in peace, and may God go with you. Christ Jesus take you by the hand, and the Spirit be a cloud of grace around you.
All:	**Amen.**

Index of themes

(This index is not exhaustive; it indicates places where the particular theme is treated at some length. Many of the themes recur throughout the book.)

Index of resources for worship